PRAISE FOR LITTLE LIFE WORDS

It takes a wise, tender, and frankly, pierced heart to write the words that Jenny Gehman has in these pages. Deftly weaving together Scripture, personal reflection, practice, humor, and sorrow, Jenny offers invitation after invitation to sit down, drop your heavy load, be warmed and well fed, and perhaps begin haltingly and in a holy way to tell your own story to God. For me, as one who both leads others and also struggles to find the space and the invitation to let down, Jenny's words have been a sweet reminder of Life.

— TARA OWENS, CSD, CSDS; EXECUTIVE
DIRECTOR, ANAM CARA MINISTRIES; AUTHOR,
EMBRACING THE BODY

This book is a timely offering for all who are navigating through the beautiful, rough, raw terrain of life. I cried (good tears) my way through most of it!

— JENNIE GROFF, SOCIAL ENTERPRISE
BUSINESS LEADER

You hold in your hands a treasure chest filled with wisdom, understanding, and hard-won insight. Jenny is a wise and compassionate guide for your soul.

— BECKY GRISELL, DMIN, LEADERSHIP AND
SPIRITUAL FORMATION

I have been looking for a book of meditations that is generous and generative, one that doesn't offer platitudes nor shy away from the hard places. Jenny has written what I've been looking for: meditations that invite us to linger in the capacious love of God, to ponder both Scripture and our own lives, offering simple yet creative practices to engage the promptings of the Spirit as one carries the meditation into their week. Jenny's writing is both invitational and grounding, spacious and encouraging. *Little Life Words* is a gentle and kind companion that I look forward to sharing with loved ones and directees alike.

— ELIZABETH PETERSON, SPIRITUAL
DIRECTOR; MA, SPIRITUAL FORMATION

Little Life Words is a true gem. Each time I sit down to read one of the meditations, my heart and spirit are calmed by these small, thoughtful nuggets of care. I've never read just one at a time—they gently beckon me to keep reading, offering comfort and insight with every word.

— CYNEATHA MILLSAPS, EXECUTIVE
DIRECTOR, MENNONITE WOMEN USA;
EXECUTIVE DIRECTOR, GOSHEN COLLEGE
CENTER FOR COMMUNITY ENGAGEMENT

Little Life Words does not disappoint. In these well written and engaging meditations, Jenny masterfully weaves familiar Scriptures into personal stories and/or reflections, making them come alive in new ways. I can easily see how a sermon could be developed by using each meditation as a germination point.

— DANIEL GRIMES, RETIRED, VICE PRESIDENT
FOR ADVANCEMENT AND ENROLLMENT,
ANABAPTIST MENNONITE BIBLICAL SEMINARY

Gehman's gentle writing encourages us to pause and reflect, offering supportive insights as we navigate the roller coaster of life with love and grace. This book is a heartfelt invitation to deepen your connection with yourself, God, and the world around you.

— DR. NELSON OKANYA, PRESIDENT, WORLD
SERVING LEADERS

Little Life Words is like being served a small plate at a Michelin-starred restaurant, where each bite is meant to be savored and the experience lingers far beyond the moment. Though easily digestible in a few minutes' time, Jenny challenges the reader to allow the content to simmer. What results is inspiration, conviction, and transformation, where one can't help but want to return for more.

— DEBBIE WENGER

Jenny's little words guide us in our relationship with a big God through creative discoveries in Scripture linked to everyday life experiences.

— KEITH YODER, MINISTRY AND LEADERSHIP CONSULTANT

God has given Jenny a way with words that speak right to the heart of the reader. With messages of hope, peace, love, and joy, *Little Life Words* will be read and shared over and over again, nourishing and encouraging the soul.

— BRINTON CULP

Connecting life's joys and struggles with truths from Scripture, Jenny condenses big ideas into a few words, making her practical encouragement memorable.

— PAUL SCHRAG, EDITOR, *ANABAPTIST WORLD*

Gehman's fresh yet simple reflections and embodiment practices reveal the deep and abiding truth that we are being loved and cared for by a good God. This book is an invitation into the satisfying and sustaining relationship with our Creator that we are all longing for.

— MAILE SILVA, CO-OWNER, NOOKS BOOKSTORE, LANCASTER, PENNSYLVANIA

I'm thrilled to have this entire collection of Jenny's *Little Life Words* to hold in my hand and peruse at my leisure. One of the things I love most about this book is its accessibility. Each meditation's theme is clear and concise, boiled down to its very essence, making it easy to carry those words and ideas with me throughout my day and allow them to sink into my soul. Steeped in the reality of everyday life, I always find something meaningful: a challenge, a balm, an affirmation, a question to ponder, an alternative point of view to consider. If you're searching for life and hope—and aren't we all, in these fast-paced and complicated days—*Little Life Words* is the perfect traveling companion.

— KATHY SWAAR, MA; AUTHOR, *FINE LINES*
AND *SOPHIE*

With a humble heart and comfortable tone, Jenny's *Little Life Words* is like a relaxed conversation next to a warm fireplace. Her keen insight and encouraging words will challenge and guide you as you ponder more of God's hidden truths and sacred nuggets.

— DAN SIGMON, PASTOR OF CARE

Little Life Words is a beautiful invitation to the seeking soul. Each meditation will draw you into the presence of Jesus, where you will find strength and peace for this journey we call life!

— ANITA KEAGY, FOUNDER, JOYSHOP
MINISTRIES; AUTHOR, *THE FILE* AND *SEEKING
GOD FIRST*

Little Life Words is a wonderful collection of devotions that share vulnerability, joy, sorrow, and love. Jenny's willingness to share from her heart is refreshing. I highly recommend this book.

— CHRISTINE SINE, AUTHOR, *THE GIFT OF WONDER*; HOST, *LITURGICAL REBELS* PODCAST

These little life words are everything I didn't know I needed to hear. It's like your friend is sitting right beside you, sharing wisdom over steaming cups of tea. Jenny invites you to know God more by listening and looking for him in all the moments of your life—no matter how little.

— JENNIFER BALMER

LITTLE LIFE WORDS

60 MEDITATIONS TO SOOTHE, CENTER, AND STRENGTHEN YOUR SOUL

JENNY GEHMAN

To my sweet mom, who lived to see the day!
You've always been my everything.
I love you!
—Jennifer Joy

The Sovereign Lord has given me a well-instructed tongue,
to know the word that sustains the weary.
He wakens me morning by morning,
wakens my ear to listen like one being instructed.
—Isaiah 50:4, NIV

CONTENTS

FOREWORD

After years of following Jenny Gehman's writing, I loved seeing how this new book, *Little Life Words*, begins with a prayer for the reader that perfectly articulates both the voice and heart that attracted me to her work in the first place: "May God's comfort and care be upon you." This line of prayer summarizes the essence of this book and the heart of the author and soul shepherd who has poured herself into each page of it. Jenny writes for the sake of bringing God's comfort and care to her reader's soul through these little, though large, life words. Within these pages you will be nourished by one who has been uniquely gifted with warmth and wisdom and who is motivated by the simple desire to bring daily morsels of both to you, her beloved reader.

This book is one to be moved through slowly and would make a perfect morning devotional read. Each segment offers a short reflection with a corresponding mantra and set of questions and prayers that can be marinated on throughout the day. I also love the creative practices that accompany each section, which would be really great to do with friends.

One of my favorite portions in this book is titled "Gracious Gifts." There, Jenny wrote about someone telling her that her name meant "gracious gift from God." After that interaction, Jenny wondered, "And what if we all knew this? What if it was conferred on each of us, regardless of our given names? What if we acted on it in humility, not haughtiness, offering ourselves to one another as gifts of grace? A gift, freely given for the benefit of the other."

I love that section because I often wonder this myself. What would come of the world if we could all get back to really knowing this? And the best way, and maybe the only way, is for that knowing to be conferred upon us by others who have come to know it themselves and who have then begun to offer themselves up to others as blessings in response. Which is exactly what Jenny does in this book. It's a gracious gift of personal story, sharp insight, and kindhearted invitation to lean into the blessing of this life with God a little more every day ourselves.

—KAREN MILIOTO, author; regenerative farmer;
MA, Christian spiritual formation and leadership

TO THE READER

I'm deeply honored you've chosen to pick up or purchase this book. You are holding my heart in your hands.

I want to begin by bowing to you, dear reader, as I welcome you into these pages. I have so many hopes for you, and whispered prayers have already left my lips on your behalf. May God's comfort and care be upon you, and may you find courage for the living of these days.

Every single one of the words in this book first arrived as a tender gift from God to me in my own times of need. This is me simply sharing them with you.

I have a room in my home—a renovated closet, to be exact, to which I retreat in the predawn hours of my days. My family has named this room the SS *Jenny*, as if I board a ship each sunrise. The S's stand for Sacred Space, which has also now become my safe, settled, and sought-after space. It is here these words, all of them, come to visit me while in prayer.

The SS *Jenny* holds a chair, a table, and a dresser from my grandparents' home. Four lanterns hang on the walls, casting their warm, welcoming glow. And in the corner of this room, you will find a campfire. Real wood, real stone, but my husband (wise man that he is) drew the line at real flame. The low light comes instead from a salt lamp, sent by my sister, sitting at its base.

This campfire does more than cast light. It speaks to me of a story found in John 21. Jesus's disciples were having a rough go of it at the time. They were reeling from his recent death, from the betrayal and loss of their friend Judas, and from their own foibles and failures. Now they spent their days locked up in fear. When they finally risked leaving their four walls to return to fishing, they failed even in that. Nothing was working the way they imagined.

Into this scene comes the risen Christ, a campfire, and a call to come home. Jesus made them breakfast, and that makes me cry. It is this kind of hospitality that heals me.

It is here, sitting around these stones in my sacred space, that I spill my own stories. It is this welcoming presence of Jesus that soothes me, centers me, and strengthens my own soul.

ABOUT THIS BOOK

Inside, you will find sixty contemplative meditations. Sixty, because this first book of mine is being released in my sixtieth year. Each of the meditations are followed by questions for you to ponder, spiritual practices for you to engage, and a suggested prayer.

This book has been slow-cooked and simmered, having been written over a five-year stretch. It is my hope you will receive it in the same way—that it might be for you a slow steep, not a speed read. I would invite you to sit down in each meditation for a week or so, allowing the words to have their way with you, to find their way in you. Perhaps you'd like to read it in the style of *lectio divina*, a slow and sacred reading.

One possible suggestion:

- **Day 1:** Read the meditation (out loud, if possible) and simply receive it. Let it wash over you. Begin praying the suggested prayer.
- **Day 2:** Read again, taking time to reflect on one or more of the Ponder questions.

- **Day 3:** As you read, notice a word or phrase that stands out to you. Meditate on how it may apply to some part of your life today. Begin to engage in the suggested practice.
- **Day 4:** Read and notice God's invitation to you from this meditation. In what way might you respond?
- **Day 5:** Read and rest, allowing the goodness and graces God has brought to sink down deep.

You will notice throughout these meditations that I use male pronouns for God. I trust you and I implore you, dear reader, to please substitute whatever language allows you to safely open to and move toward this God who loves you so.

You may also notice I reference some Scripture stories more than once, each time from a different perspective or point of view. For me, Scripture is always new, as the Holy Spirit highlights fresh truth for me even within the same words. I hope it will be the same for you.

You need not read these meditations in order or finish within a certain time frame—or goodness, finish at all. You need not answer every question, engage each practice, or pray all the prayers. You are free to come and to go, to take and to leave. I do hope you'll linger long.

Be well, dear reader. May all God's graces be yours.

BOW TO BEGIN

PRAYER: May I bow to begin.

My husband was a square dancer back in the day. I've heard it was one of the ways a nice Mennonite boy could find himself a gal. But alas, I was on the disco floor.

While square dance didn't bring us together, it does keep us from falling apart. One move in particular: Bow to your partner.

To the best of my knowledge (which is admittedly small in this area), the aforementioned move is the very first call of every square dance. You begin with a bow.

This is wisdom I want to waltz with all the way home.

I wonder what might happen if I adopt this practice in my daily life. If I pause at the start of anything and everything—this day, this person, this work, this plan—to greet it with a bow. I wonder if I might enjoy the dance more than when I charge right in with two left feet, a tangled, tripping mess.

To bow is to approach with reverence and honor and a

healthy dose of respect. I am finding that, when implemented, this approach de-escalates both me and the person or project with whom I am about to engage.

I've often heard there's only one thing we can really control in life, and that's our attitude. But I think I may have stumbled onto one more (and who's not looking for more things to control?). I think we get to control our approach—the way we move toward and begin to engage with people, projects, and, yes, even problems and pain. We can bow to begin.

I was reading in 1 Peter 1 the other day when verse 17 caught my heart: "Conduct yourselves with true reverence throughout the time of your temporary residence [on the earth, whether long or short]" (AMPC).

The words *true reverence* and *temporary residence* stood out to me. I want to live my residence on Earth in reverence to God and all God has made. A deep bow to creation and all of its creatures.

This isn't easy, dear reader. When I'm in a rush, there's little time for reverence. I plow through my day without pause, and may the Lord have pity on the partner before me! And then, let's be honest, there are simply some people I don't want to bow before: those with whom the dance is awkward at best, due to failed attempts in the past. How might it be different if I began with a bow?

O God, may we live as if we are standing on holy ground because, as it turns out, we are. May our days be bookended with bows.

PONDER

How do you typically approach your day, your work, your people, your God?

What might change if you were to take one moment of reverential pause before engaging who or what is before you —each new person, problem, project, or pain?

What or who do you hope to approach differently?

PRACTICE

Physically bow to begin. Even if, for you, it looks like a small head nod, bow this day before those you meet, before you begin your work, before God, before engaging difficult conversations. Bow to begin.

PRAY

Holy Spirit, grant me the grace to bow to begin.

2

DO WHAT MATTERS MOST

Prayer: May I do what matters most.

I'm a morning person, but years ago, there was a day when I rolled out of bed only to feel every ounce of energy drain from my body. I had no way to retrieve it, nothing to go on, and a whole day ahead of me.

Defeated and depleted, I plopped down on the chest at the foot of my bed. That's when the Holy Spirit sidled up next to me and whispered sweet somethings in my ear. "Do what leads to life," was what I heard.

I scrawled the instructions on a piece of paper and tucked them in my back pocket as a reminder. All day long, one step at a time, the Spirit (and the scrawling) reminded me to do what leads to life: take a nap, phone a friend, let it go, go outside, give thanks, find beauty, count to ten, cry my tears. Do what leads to life.

This little mantra has seen me through some five thousand days, and I am grateful. Today, a new mantra arrived: "Do what matters most."

I've been thinking a good bit about the word *matter*. One way I can tell what matters to me is by how much space I give it in my life. I was recently engaged in a creative project that took up so much room in my schedule, it elbowed other things and people to the periphery. Should it have? Especially when I suspect it wasn't the project as much as my perfectionism that mattered so much?

My mind turns to Jesus addressing the religious leaders on what was, to him, no small matter. He minced no words: "You are obsessed with peripheral issues. . . . These matters are fine, yet you ignore the most important duties of all: to walk in the love of God, to display mercy to others, and to live with integrity. Readjust your values and place first things first" (Matt. 23:23, TPT).

For me, readjusting values requires readjusting vision.

When I go to the ophthalmologist, the technician lowers a machine before my eyes and asks me to look through a series of lenses at small letters posted across the room. "Which is clearer, A or B?" she asks as she clicks through the lenses. "And how about now, A or B?" We do this a dozen or so times.

This experience is what comes to mind now. It's as if I'm sitting with Jesus while he clicks through a series of situations and scenarios and asks me, "What matters more, Jenny, A or B?" Click, click, click. "And how about now?" Click, click, click.

We do this, Jesus and me, until I can see more clearly. It's not just what matters; it's what matters most.

Jesus, help us to know, and to choose, that which matters most.
Pull us from the periphery back into presence—to do justice,
love mercy, and walk humbly with you, our God.

PONDER

What does how you spend your time and money have to say about what matters most to you?

What peripheral issues might you be obsessed with?

What do you think matters most to God?

PRACTICE

Ask a trusted friend or family member what they think matters most to you. Then ask them why they think that.

Read through the book of Mark in the Bible and ask yourself, as you read, what seems to have mattered most to Jesus.

Take a piece of scrap paper and write "Do what matters most" on it. Slip it in your pocket or post it above your desk as a reminder.

PRAY

Healer of our eyes, adjust my vision, that I may do what matters most.

BE WITH WHAT IS

PRAYER: *Help me to be with what is.*

I n 2004, I was dragged, kicking and screaming, into a land of loss. Into a diminished and restricted place of chronic pain and isolation. For months on end, I wept as I pleaded with God to give me my life back. "I don't want to live here" was my constant cry.

During those years, God spoke to me out of Jeremiah 29. Not from the well-known "I have good plans for you" verse, but rather the ten verses that precede it. The verses containing a letter from God to the exiles. A letter which reads an awful lot like, "Dear people: I know you don't want to live here. I know it's hard. I know you want out. But precious, beloved people, this is where you live now. Therefore, I want you to build your houses, plant your gardens, have your babies. Make this place prosper."

Goodness gracious, God! This place? Really?

I took this as an invitation not only to continue to live but to learn to live well in the very place of my resistance. To open and not close. To fully be where I actually was.

That last part was the kicker: to fully be where I actually was.

This was not my natural way of being in the world. My perfectionistic and pain-avoidant parts were loud in protest. I wanted to escape what was, deny what was. Run from, hide from, or numb what was, not be with it.

That said, all these years later, I find when I am able to live into this, it is a healing way of saying yes to whatever and whomever is there. Yes to the truth of it, without the need to fight, flee, fashion, or fix.

It is an act of hospitality. A gift of presence to that which has walked through my door, bidden or not. A stance of welcome to the actual, and only, life I have.

Jesus, when you had to be with the terrible truth of what was coming, you asked your friends to draw near and keep watch with you. They fell asleep. They ran away. It's hard to be with what is. Have mercy on us. Stay with us, we pray.

PONDER

When Adam and Eve hid in the garden, God called them and asked, "Where are you?" Let's answer that question: Where are you? Describe your life as it is right now.

Where in your life are you feeling resistance and engaging in fight, flight, or fix-it mode?

Who or what might help you to be with what is right now?

PRACTICE

Pray the Welcoming Prayer by Father Thomas Keating.

Find a small way to make a painful place prosper. Perhaps bring beauty to it through artwork, poetry, or a live plant. Maybe take a photo of one good thing, and frame it where it will find you throughout your day. Or consider beginning each hard day with a nice, deep breath, a short walk, or a warm drink of some kind.

PRAY

Ever-present God, help me to be with what is.

4

NIGHT WATCHMEN

PRAYER: Watch over me in the dark.

Night watchmen. That's the role the shepherds were assigned on the night of Jesus's birth, "keeping watch over their flocks at night" (Luke 2:8, NIV). They were guarding and protecting, as night watchmen do. Staying awake to what lurked in the dark.

What a tender gift to have someone watch over you as darkness descends!

Nearing the end of his life, Jesus invited Peter, James, and John to keep watch with him as night closed in around him. "My soul is overwhelmed with sorrow to the point of death," he told them. "Stay here and keep watch with me" (Matt. 26:38, NIV). But try as they may, they fell asleep and failed him.

We are human, all. It is difficult to stay awake to the kind of pain that puts the lights right out. We know this.

But there is more in the dark than we might expect. "My soul waits for the Lord to break into the world," the psalmist proclaimed, "more than night watchmen expect the break of day, even more than night watchmen expect the break of day" (Ps. 130:6, VOICE).

This verse fascinates me. Most night watchmen in this day and age are posted to prevent break-ins. But in this scenario, we have watchmen longing for one, looking for God's breaking into this world. And didn't those shepherds back at Jesus's birth, staring into the inky darkness, see just that?

The dark of night is prime time for most break-ins—apparently God's included! "You know very well," Jesus told his disciples, "that the day of the Lord is going to come like a thief in the night" (1 Thess. 5:2, CEB).

This makes me wonder if one of the things lurking in the dark is the love of God about to break through. What if as we stay awake to the pain, we are also privileged to see God's presence?

As a spiritual director, one of my roles and greatest gifts is to serve as a night watchman in this way. To stay awake to and with my directees in their dark nights. Present to the pain and the presence of God, both—for the night watchmen are not only posted to prevent break-ins, but also to proclaim them. God has come!

Jesus Christ, light in the darkness, thief in the night, break in upon us. Steal away our sorrow, sin, and shame, and leave us with your peace once more.

PONDER

Who has watched over you in the dark night of your soul,

staying awake to both your pain and the presence of God in your life?

In what ways have you seen God break in during dark nights? Has it felt more like tiptoes or bright lights?

Who in your life might need a night watchman right now? How can you wait (in hope) with them?

PRACTICE

Purchase a pair of inexpensive night-vision glasses. Put them on in prayer, and ask God to help you see in the dark.

Take yourself outside in the dark. Behold the beauty that is there.

PRAY

Good Shepherd, watch over me in the dark.

5

HELD FAST

PRAYER: Hold me fast.

Hold fast. It's a term that traces back to Norwegian and Dutch sailors of old who were in such need of its reminder, they had a practice of tattooing it onto the four front-facing knuckles of each hand. This served as a constant reminder that while they held the lines in stormy seas, they would not let go. Ever. No matter what. Their lives depended on it.

Their lives depended on it, but do ours?

I've begun thinking about all the things I hold fast to and have realized that, like the sailors of old, I take a white-knuckle approach out of fear. And more accurately, out of fear of loss, especially in stormy weather.

When fear levels rise, most of us clamp down in control. White-knuckling our rights, our beliefs, our space, our status. Doubling down on our religion, relationships, and resources. So much fear of so much loss has us holding on, grip over grasp. We hold fast out of fear.

What if we let go? What if we could trust? What if, instead of writing HOLD FAST on our knuckles, we changed one little letter—the O to an E? What if instead of HOLD we wrote HELD?

HELD FAST. What then? What if we tattooed *this* on our knuckles so every time we're tempted to grip, grasp, or hold on fast, we might be reminded to relax. To release. To relinquish to the One who holds us all?

"He holds you firmly in place," the psalmist says of God. "He will not let you fall. He who keeps you will never take His eyes off you and never drift off to sleep. What a relief!" (Ps. 121:3–4, VOICE).

God, our muscles are tired and tense from all the holding on, holding together, holding up, and holding fast. We think we've gotten this wrong. So loosen our grip, even as you hold us in your grasp. You are the one who never lets go.

PONDER

To what or to whom are you holding fast?

Do you prefer being the one who holds or the one who is held? Why?

PRACTICE

Pull out your pen and write HELD FAST on your knuckles. Let it serve as a reminder through your week (and quite a good conversation starter!).

PRAY

You who keep me, hold me fast.

6

SLACK OFF!

Prayer: Cut me some slack.

I n Psalm 46, we hear the writer vividly describe a world falling apart—mountains crumbling, waters roaring, nations raging—and us invited to be still. That's quite a juxtaposition!

"Be still, and know that I am God," the writer records God speaking into the madness and mayhem (v. 10, NIV). This feels like a too-tall order.

The Passion translation words this verse, "Surrender your anxiety," which feels like an even taller order, given the circumstances. It further footnotes that the big, little word of *still* means to let go. Now, I'm thinking there's no way on God's green earth that's going to happen.

This invitation is issued into a scenario in which I'd rather grip, grasp, and hold on fast! Letting go is the last thing on my list when the earth moves under my feet. But there it is, all the same.

"Be still" doesn't mean to freeze in fear. Nor does it imply we sit quietly, with hands folded calmly in our laps. Rather, it is an invitation to sink into, to relax, to slacken.

Slacken. There it is. This word intrigues me. *Slacken,* dear reader, means to slow, to become gradually less strong—yes, you read that right—less intense, less tight. And in the midst of all that is falling apart!

This requires a boatload of trust. But I'm finding it truly can be good news to those of us who have had to be so very strong for so very long. We don't have to hold it all. Permission to slack off.

Sink, slacken, and surrender your anxiety—for God is God, and God is near, ready to help at break of day (v. 5).

The entirety of Psalm 46 tells us God is our shelter, strength, stronghold, and place of safety. It is this we can sink into. It is here we can slack off. Here, we can surrender not only our anxieties, but also our sense of insufficient, try-so-hard, have-to-muster-it-all-up strength.

God, we are tired and too often fearful. Help us to see that in the midst of madness and mayhem, there is you. Always a still center, and never slacking off.

PONDER

Today's Scripture says to "be still [slacken] and know." What "knowing" would enable you to slack off for a while?

What fears arise as you think about becoming "gradually less strong"?

PRACTICE

Try engaging in the practice of progressive muscle relaxation to experience a slackening, or lessening tension, in your body.

Find a decent thickness of rope, and tie a tight knot in it. Each day this week, loosen that knot just a little bit. As you do, pray for your own loosening and letting go as well.

PRAY

God of mercy, cut me some slack.

7

PEACED TOGETHER

PRAYER: Peace me together.

We are held together by peace. Quite literally, we are "peaced" together, as if stitched like a quilt.

There are several words for *peace* in the Scriptures. The one we may know best is *shalom*. But I want to focus on another: *eiréné*. Defined as wholeness, it means when all essential parts, as in a patchwork quilt, are joined together. It's the opposite of being pulled apart.

When a woman, long-suffering with a situation unsolved, came to Jesus to steal a healing, he called her out. She wasn't going to get away without a blessing. *"Eiréné,"* he spoke to her. *Peace.*

"Daughter," he said, with I'd imagine tender awe in his voice, "your faith has healed you. Go in peace [go in *eiréné*] and be freed from your suffering" (Mark 5:34, NIV).

Be freed from that which has fragmented you. Yes, please.

I love the wording the Amplified Bible uses in this

passage. Instead of simply saying to go in peace, it says go *into* peace. As if it's waiting right there for you.

May you go into a place where you're pulled together and not apart. And may you be freed from your suffering.

I think of the strong admonishment often issued to us in anxious hours, that we need to pull it together. Meaning, we need to clamp down and calm down and control our frightened feelings.

But what if we don't need to pull it together ourselves as much as we need to be "peaced" together by another? What if the fragments are too far flung for us to gather on our own? Might the God who knit us together in the first place (Ps. 139) "peace" us together now?

"God made my life complete," the psalmist once said, "when I placed all the pieces before him" (Ps. 18:20, MSG). May it be so.

Jesus, I'm struck by the fact that after you fed the crowd of five thousand, you had your disciples collect the fragments. They collected the fragments and brought them to you. And so we do the same. We wander here and there in prayer, bringing this piece and that of our lives, our communities, and our world to you. All the broken-off bits. Peace us together, we pray. Make us whole once more.

PONDER

What is pulling you apart?

What parts need to be "peaced" together?

What pieces of your life, hopes, dreams, work, communities, and the like might you gather up and place before God this week?

PRACTICE

As a daily act of prayer this week, present your pieces to God.

Go for a walk and collect fragments, little bits and bobs, and then make something of them.

Try your hand at quilting, stitching pieces together.

PRAY

God of peace, peace me together.

8

CALL TO MIND

Prayer: Come to my side.

I have a spiritual practice that helps to ground and keep me in unprecedented times, and it is this: Call to mind.

I found this little gem in the middle of a small book of the Bible. A small book with some very big feelings: the book of Lamentations. The entire book is a loud outpouring of grief as God's people face wave upon wave of unrelenting sorrow and loss.

It's a tough read, but it's given me this important practice, because smack-dab in the middle of the grief, the writer makes a pivotal move. He calls something to mind. Calls it to come—as if it weren't there, as if it had run off and left and was no longer within his reach.

He calls something to mind. Listen in:

"I have been deprived of peace; I have forgotten what prosperity is. So I say, 'My splendor is gone and all that I had hoped from the LORD.' I remember my affliction and my wandering, the bitterness and the gall. I well remember them, and my soul is downcast within me. *Yet this I call to mind* and therefore I have hope: Because of the LORD's great love we are not consumed, for his compassions never fail. They are new every morning; great is your faithfulness" (Lam. 3:17–23, emphasis added, NIV).

"Yet this I call to mind." Did you hear it?

It's like when your dog gets away from you and you whistle and bend down low and pat your leg while calling its name to come and be by you and with you and companion you once more. You're calling him to come.

That's what I picture when I hear the writer's words in Lamentations here. Calling something to mind to come and companion him once more. Something that had gotten away from him for one reason or another. Something like hope.

It's not lost on me that the writer remembered well his affliction, pain, and suffering. Those things needed no call to accompany him. But he bent down low and called other companions close: love, compassion, mercy, and the faithfulness of God.

Can you see them run to him like a beloved pet? Full-out speed, ears flapping, tail wagging, jumping into his arms, and licking his face? Yes!

God, when all seems lost and hope has strayed, help us to call to mind your great love and mercy made new. Return them to us, we pray.

PONDER

What is accompanying you?

What has left you?

What do you need to call to mind?

PRACTICE

Follow Paul's example in Philippians 4:8. Call to mind "the best, not the worst; the beautiful, not the ugly; things to praise, not things to curse" (MSG). Go on a daily treasure hunt for these, and find a way to document or share what you find.

PRAY

God of hope, come to my side.

9

COME FOR US

PRAYER: Come for me.

"Comfort us!" I cried. And who isn't crying it these days? What other prayer can even be on our lips? I tugged on God's sleeve, asking God to grant such comfort to myself and to the masses. For near and dear, for friends and strangers far away.

As I prayed this over and over again, something surprising began to happen. I heard those two words in a new way. Not as "comfort us" but "come *for* us."

And I thought, "Yes. Yes! Come for your people, O God! Come for your people. Don't leave us alone in the depth of this dark."

One of the times I experienced this kind of comfort was in January 2017. At that time, my siblings and I were camped out in the waiting room of the ICU while our mother fought for her life. Our dad had died just a few days earlier. We had come to this hospital in Maryland from multiple places—

Virginia, Pennsylvania, and Washington state—to keep her alive and see each other through.

We huddled near the entrance, and I still remember when those doors to the blustery outside slid open and my cousins, whom we had grown up with, walked through them. Tears of gratitude mingled with my grief at their arrival.

We had come for Mom, but they had come for us. Pulling chairs into a circle, we lingered there. In that place of fear and unknowing, we shared stories, silences, and snacks. And by their coming, we were comforted.

Comfort comes when we are come for.

If God does anything, God does this! It is the one persistent promise of God's presence, that God will move ever toward us and never away.

As I continued my prayer for comfort, I experienced an unanticipated reversal. God began to tug on my sleeve as I had tugged on his: "'Comfort, O comfort My people,' says your God" (Isa. 40:1, AMP).

As I implored God, God cried it right back to me. "Come for us!" I pleaded. "Go to them!" God urged.

"[God] comforts [comes alongside] us in all our troubles, so that we can comfort those in any trouble with the comfort we ourselves receive from God" (2 Cor. 1:4, NIV).

Come for your people, O God, come for your people. Come for and comfort, we pray.

PONDER

Who has come for you?

How, when, or where have you experienced God as the "God of all comfort" (2 Cor. 1:3, NIV)?

PRACTICE

Think of someone who needs coming for, and show up in their lives this week by sending a card, making a call, sending flowers, or bringing food.

PRAY

God of all comfort, come for me.

10

STAND BY ME

Prayer: Stand by me.

"I will not let you face this alone." So said my sister in a show of solidarity.

I was in the midst of a rather excruciating year when my mother and I flew out to Washington state to visit my sister, Christy. The three of us were just pulling into the parking lot to tour some peaceful Japanese gardens when I received a troubling phone call.

Before I could perceive what was happening, my sister had pulled into a parking space, stopped the car, and began climbing over her children's car seats to reach me in the rear of the van. Tears streamed down my face. She sat there by my side, holding my hand. "I will not let you face this alone," she said.

My sister could not fix the situation. She could not wish it or pray it away. Could not spare me from it. But she could do one thing. She could enter it. And so she did.

I don't think I'll ever forget the moment she broke into

my world and my pain in such a simple and profound way. Just to be with me.

And here's what I'm noticing: God is a good bit like my sister.

We see it when the apostle Paul was in prison, facing possible death, and feeling very much alone.

"At my first defense, no one came to my support," Paul lamented to his friend Timothy. "Everyone deserted me" (2 Tim. 4:16, NIV). Then he went on to say, "But the Lord stood by my side and gave me strength" (v. 17, NIV).

The Lord stood by his side and gave him strength. Just like my sister did for me. And just like my sister, God climbs over obstacles and bypasses barriers to reach us wherever we are. "I won't let you face this alone," God says, as he takes our hands and holds us tight.

God, your one consistent promise is that you will be with us. That you will never leave us. That we won't have to face anything alone. So climb over the obstacles and bypass the barriers to reach us right where we are.

PONDER

What are you facing? What do you need?

In another Scripture, Paul recorded that during a shipwreck, God's angel stood at his side and said, "Do not be afraid" (Acts 27:24, NIV). Imagine Jesus or an angel coming to stand by your side. What do they give you? What do they say?

PRACTICE

When Paul told Timothy about those who had not stood by him, he went on to say, "May it not be held against them" (2 Tim. 4:16, NIV). Is there anyone who has failed you in this way? Anyone by whom you feel deserted? What might it be like to name the truth of this and then release them as Paul did?

Write a thank-you note to someone who has stood by your side.

PRAY

Present One, stand by me.

11

CALM AND COURAGEOUS

PRAYER: Keep me calm. Grant me courage.

At the end of Jesus's earthly life, he gave a farewell gift to his understandably distraught disciples. The gift was peace. And it was no small offering.

"I leave the gift of peace with you," he said. "Not the kind of fragile peace given by the world, but my perfect peace. Do not let your heart be troubled, nor let it be afraid. Let my perfect peace calm you in every circumstance and give you courage and strength for every challenge" (John 14:27, TPT, AMP).

This is no fragile peace, Jesus said, for it contains the power to produce both calmness and courage. Not just sometimes but, if he was right (and I have a sneaking suspicion he was), for every circumstance and every challenge.

The disciples had heard this word of peace before. In fact, they'd seen it in action a time or two. They were in the boat when Jesus spoke it to the wind and waves, and they saw for themselves the calmness that ensued. They knew about this peace, saw how it governed Jesus's own life, and now it would be theirs. *Theirs!*

Jesus knows how to give good gifts.

To be calm means to be free from agitation, undisturbed, steady and still. To be courageous is to be undeterred, having the mental or moral strength to persevere in the face of fear or difficulty.

Undeterred and *undisturbed*. In a nutshell, these are the gifts Jesus gives, wrapped in the package of peace. A power to face all that is right now and all that is to come.

If I could, I'd take your hands and place this peace into them, curl your fingers around it so you'd have it to hold and so it would hold you.

"Be calm and courageous," I'd whisper. "Christ's peace will keep you still."

God, we stand with hands outstretched and hearts wide open. Place in us, please, this peace you've promised, that we may be undeterred and undisturbed by any and all that rages round us this day. We need you every hour.

PONDER

What is troubling your heart or causing it to be afraid?

Which do you need more of right now, the gift of being undisturbed or undeterred? Why?

PRACTICE

Practice blessing others—friends, enemies, and strangers

alike—with this silent or spoken prayer: *The peace of Christ be with your spirit.*

Open your hands in prayer. Imagine God giving you calm for this day's circumstances, courage for this day's challenges.

PRAY

Peace-giving God, keep me calm; grant me courage.

12

GRACIOUS GIFT

PRAYER: Call me by name.

I went to our neighborhood polling place during local elections. Stepping up to the registration table, I gave my name to the petite, gray-haired woman smiling up at me from the opposite side. After locating me on her list, she spoke my name back to me in the form of a question.

"Jennifer?" Then, with a glint in her eye, she asked if I knew what my name meant.

Before I could answer, she proceeded to tell me: "It means gracious gift from God."

I always thought my name meant Fair One, but who was I to argue? I accepted the grace she offered, did my civic duty, and headed home.

But the interaction lingered, refusing to leave me.

I asked Google the meaning of my name. As I suspected, it's Fair One. And yet I could not dismiss this interaction. That woman conferred a blessing on me, calling me a gracious gift from God, and I felt the holiness of it when it happened. Like bowing. Like bending. Like removing my shoes.

Right there in the lobby of our local polling place, a gift was given on holy ground. I don't want to wear it in a haughty, "I'm God's gift to the world" kind of way. But the truth is, I am. And so are you.

And what if we all knew this? What if it was conferred on each of us, regardless of our given names? What if we acted on it in humility, not haughtiness, offering ourselves to one another as gifts of grace, a gift freely given for the benefit of the other?

I've been named a thing or three in my lifetime, and not all of them have landed like anointing oil or a kiss on the cheek. Some names landed hard, like a crushing weight pressing me down. Some names have come from others. Some, off my very own lips.

We live into our names, and too often in a negative way: unwanted, unworthy, not right, not enough. I want to live into this new name—to be a gift and a grace to those I meet. And I'd like to call others to do the same.

What if we went around naming one another as good? As gifts? And what if we received each other as the good and gracious gifts we are? What if each time someone came our way, our spirit inwardly jumped up and down, saying, "Here comes a good and gracious gift"? Can you imagine?

I wish I would have stuck around the polling place a little longer. I have a sneaking suspicion that little old lady knew the meaning of the name of each person who came her way. I can hear her now: "What's your name, dear? Amanda? Martin? Phyllis? Peter? Do you know what your name means? It means gracious gift from God."

God who calls the stars by name, name us, too, we pray.
Name us good, name us gift, name us as grace in this world.

PONDER

What negative names have you been called by others or by yourself? To what effect?

By what name do you long to be called, and why?

PRACTICE

Look for the gift in another, and then name to them the gift that they are.

Literally jump up and down in delight when you see someone. Notice their response.

Research what your given name means.

Look in the mirror and name it out loud: "I am a good gift from God."

PRAY

You who know me, call me by name.

13

BE AND BRING

PRAYER: Help me to bring what I have.

There were more than five thousand hungry people at the unplanned picnic that fateful day. Five thousand people, but nary a bite of food. How could this be? (See John 6:1–14.)

One brave little boy surveyed his basket: five small barley loaves and two small fish. Did no one else in the entire crowd think to bring anything? Did they hoard what they had for themselves? Withhold it out of shame, knowing it too meager to match the mountainous need?

I'm curious how Jesus's disciple Andrew found the little boy in such a large crowd. Did the child step to the front—too small to know shame—and hold out what he had? If so, what prompted Andrew to take that seemingly foolish offering to Jesus, not dismissing the small child, small bread, small fish, simple faith?

Did Andrew recall that time he and others tried to bar the children from coming to Jesus for a blessing? "Jesus was irate," we're told, "and let them know it: 'Don't push these children away. Don't ever get between them and me'" (Mark 10:14, MSG).

This time, did Andrew's pride step aside as he let this little one in? Not to *be* blessed, but rather to *offer* a blessing? By doing just that, permission was given for the boy to be who he was and bring what he had. I have to wonder how this shaped the remainder of his days.

The reality is, we're not always who others want us to be. Goodness, we're not always who *we* want us to be, either. But in God's kingdom, we are invited, time and again, to be entirely who we are and to bring whatever we have to give.

I think of the woman at the well, invited to give Jesus a drink (John 4:4–26). The prostitute, welcomed to wash Jesus's feet with her tears and wipe them with her hair (Luke 7:36–38). The widow, giving her mite (Mark 12:41–44). Mary, pouring out the prized and precious oil and Jesus's defense of her. "Leave her alone," he said. "Why do you make trouble for her? She has done a good thing for me" (Mark 14:6, CEB).

All allowed to be who they were and give what they had.

How might we become more like Andrew, one who sees the gift and doesn't despise the giver, who opens the way and ushers others in? How might we be like the little boy, unashamed to hold out what we have, no matter its size or fit for the need? May we stop preventing and start permitting, both ourselves and others, to be who we are and bring what we have.

God who receives the whole of us, help us to do the same. Give us the courage to contribute and not hold back in shame.

PONDER

What, if anything, gives you pause from being who you are or bringing what you have?

Who has seen a gift in you and opened the way for you to offer it?

PRACTICE

If you identified a person who opened the way for you, sit down and write them a thank-you note.

Ask several people in your life to name gifts they see in you. Act on using at least one of those gifts each day this week.

PRAY

Giver of all good gifts, help me to bring what I have.

14

WRAPPED IN LOVE

Prayer: Show me your love.

Hubby and I were road-tripping to a race our son was running. En route, I asked if we could stop at any yard sales along the way. Much to my dismay, there were none. However, we passed a church with a rummage-sale sign out front.

Imagine my excitement upon reading that all the clothing was a mere fifty cents. It was going to be a good day after all!

Once inside, I began going through the layers of clothing piled on tables and hung on racks. I found an adult head-to-toe giraffe suit, which I refused but just might regret; a number of tops; and what I think was the whole reason we made this trip: a spring-green pea coat. My color, my size, and, as you'll see in a moment, my gift from God.

As I took the pea coat from its hanger, I noticed the label sewn to the inside that read, "This garment's perfection in every detail can only be surpassed by she who wears it."

Well, wasn't that something! I had just been doing a little word study on dignity. On how we confer worth and value onto others. How we can put it on ourselves, as well. Possibly wear our worth like a spring-green pea coat in autumn.

And yet we don't always do that, do we? Put our worth on, that is. But now here it was, stitched right into the fabric and waiting for me.

When I later went through my box of clothes to try all of them on, I checked the pockets as I always do, because one never knows what one might find. My pea coat pocket did not disappoint. Tucked inside was an index card, folded in half, that simply read: "You Are Loved!"

God is always conferring upon us both dignity and love, telling us time and again of our great worth. Sometimes I don't hear him. Sometimes I don't believe him. And sometimes, sometimes, I slip my arms in, try it on for size, and wear that worth like the spring-green pea coat it is!

When it's cold outside, dismal or gray, remind us in a thousand ways of how you love us, O God, how you love us.

PONDER

Have you ever found an unexpected gift that seemed meant just for you? What was that like?

Name a time you felt loved by God.

What might it feel like to slip into and walk around in the love and dignity God confers on you?

PRACTICE

Wear something (like a spring-green pea coat!) that makes you feel as if you're clothed in dignity or wrapped in love.

PRAY

God of grace and goodness, show me your love.

15

DUTY AND DELIGHT

PRAYER: Help me do my duty with a spirit of delight.

Be it tending a garden, raising a child, cultivating a community, or caring for the chronically ill, caregiving of any kind can be hard work. The tasks of tending can become tedious. And if we're not careful, our sense of duty can overtake a spirit of delight.

Perhaps that's why I'm so drawn to God's words when he exclaims through the prophet Isaiah, concerning a vineyard he's tending, *"There's* something to sing about!" (Isa. 27:2, emphasis added, MSG).

I can sense God's pride and joy, especially as the Scriptures go on to describe a fine vineyard, a vineyard God waters, keeps careful watch over, and wishes well and whole (vv. 3–5).

But then, as I read on, I sense my own disappointment. For I read that this very vineyard, delighted over and diligently tended, bears briars and brambles, thistles and thorns.

And I think this should not be! All that careful care—by God, no less—and this is what it yields?

I'm frustrated and angry, not so much for God's sake, but for myself and my own experiences of the same.

Even when we cultivate with care, thorns and thistles happen. This makes me want to throw my hands up in resignation and stop doing all the hard work I'm doing with whomever or whatever I'm tending (myself very much included).

The briars and brambles can sometimes steal all my time and attention as I get lost in the weeds. It doesn't take long before a sense of duty takes over, drudge kicks in, and delight is nowhere to be found. This, of course, can happen in caregiving or cultivating of any kind.

This doesn't appear to happen with God. God seems more chill than me.

"Even if it gives me thistles and thornbushes, I'll just pull them out," God says (v. 4, MSG). God simply deals with them. They happen. They're not the whole garden. I sense God's nudge: "Don't get so uptight. Don't lose your delight."

Friend, those brambles are not the whole garden. It is still a fine vineyard, a fruitful vineyard, a vineyard beloved and lovely. Don't burn the whole thing down.

May we (may I!) hang up any grumpy gardener hats we have and tend what is ours as God does: with diligent duty, yes, but from a place of desire and with a deep, felt sense of overarching delight.

God, this cultivating and caregiving can wring us dry sometimes. In the midst of our duties and our diligence, would you call us back to delight? Lift us from the weeds to glimpse the wonder once more.

PONDER

What or whom are you tending to right now?

What are your responses to the briars and brambles, the thorns and thistles?

If your sense of duty and delight could have a conversation with each other, what might they have to say?

PRACTICE

Each day, look for and name one thing in which you delight. Extra points if it's about those things or people receiving your cultivation or care.

PRAY

Caregiving God, help me do my duty with a spirit of delight.

16

POWER OUTAGE

PRAYER: Direct my energies.

It was Lent, and I was engaging in a spiritual practice that involved meditating while meandering. Each day, I was given a different question with which to take a mile walk. My question on this particular day was: *What or who is begging for your energetic, physical, emotional, and/or spiritual output?*

Begging. It's an interesting word, isn't it? It involves insistence and a sense of urgency. Tugging. Pleading. Pressing. Wanting something, and now.

What or who is begging for something from me? As I set out on my walk, all varieties of answers began appearing in my mind: people, problems, and projects galore. I could feel them pressing in around me and jostling for my attention, not unlike the people did with Jesus in his days on Earth.

But my mile walk had just begun, so I listened longer, and another layer emerged. This time, it revealed an interior crowd. Perfectionism. People pleasing. Protecting, providing for, and proving myself.

I can see why it takes a mile to get to the gut of things.

Jesus was once being jostled by a crowd when a woman who had been bleeding for twelve years—a woman who should not have even been in the crowd, a woman out of hope and desperate for healing—lay hold of the hem of his garment. And when she did, power left him. (See Luke 8:43–48.)

Not everyone who touched Jesus received his power that day, but this woman did. And I wonder: What is tugging on the hem of my garment, for good or bad, laying hold of me and asking for an output of my energy?

Panic. Performative pressure. The desire to appease so as to preserve the peace.

How did Jesus discern to what or whom his power would go? How will I? It's a good question to take for a walk, don't you think?

Jesus, make us ever more aware of what lays hold of us with insistence and urgency. May our power, like yours, be put to good use.

PONDER

What or who is insistently asking for your output?

What is laying hold of you, draining your energy?

How will you discern to what or whom your power will go?

PRACTICE

Take the above questions for a mile walk and simply listen.

PRAY

God of purpose and power, direct my energies.

PORTION CONTROL

PRAYER: *Fill my plate.*

I know from firsthand experience what size portions are needed to feed and fuel an athlete in training, and it is no joke. At the peak of our son's running career, he would eat up to ten thousand calories a day. Much was being required of his body, which meant he needed a lot more food to fuel it.

Martin Luther once said, "I have so much to do that I shall spend the first three hours in prayer." I recognize this as Luther doing what our son did: taking in large quantities—of God and God's graces—in order to meet large demands.

When we have a lot to do, we often describe it as having a lot on our plates. It's what we say when life has dished up or dished out some difficult things. When my widowed friend with two young adult daughters learned she had terminal cancer, she had a lot on her plate.

But this statement, like a golden pancake, has a flip side as well. When we have a lot on our plate to do or to handle,

God, like a good parent, then puts a lot on our plate to provide what is needed. God dishes up large portions of mercy, wisdom, love, compassion, and strength equal to our days, to name just a few.

In other words, the more that is on my plate, the more I need on my plate. And God is up to the task.

When someone asks me how I handle all that life has dished up, my reply might well be this: "I eat!" I have no small appetite for God and all God gives.

I need to eat God's love whole, feast on his faithfulness, gobble up his goodness and grace. I partake of large portions of the peace he's serving.

The more that's *on* my plate, the more I *need* on my plate. And I'm not shy about coming back around for more.

"God has the power to provide you with more than enough of every kind of grace. That way, you will have everything you need" (2 Cor. 9:8, CEB).

Don't forget to eat.

God, this life can drain us dry 'til we're running on empty. You are our daily bread, our portion and cup, and more than enough. We come to you for the feasting, the filling, and the fueling we need. Feed us 'til we want no more.

PONDER

What is on your plate right now to do or to handle?

What do you need to partake of in order to fuel up for what life requires of you at the moment?

PRACTICE

Sometimes we engage in fasting. But right now, I recommend feasting! Your practice is simply to eat good food—and when you do, give thanks for the other provisions of God that fuel you well.

PRAY

You who are my portion, fill my plate.

18

TAKE. EAT.

PRAYER: Give us each our daily bread.

I t was Sunday morning. Again. I arrived at the church way too weary for the early hour it was. How could a whole day still lie ahead of me? I allowed the rhythms of song and prayer to carry me along.

Today would be Communion, and I felt unprepared. I sat in the pew, head bowed, hands now holding the broken bread, and the cup poured out.

"Take. Eat. This is for you," the pastor said.

Unsuspecting tears began to flow down my face. As one who provides care for others, I had expected to hear something akin to "Take. Give. This is for *them.*"

And then, in my imagination, I began to get caught up in the story of Jesus feeding the five thousand. In this story, Jesus was concerned that those in the crowd might faint if they were sent away empty—I felt I certainly would—so he provided their daily bread, the sustenance that would sustain them for what was to come. (See Matthew 14:13–21.)

And while the disciples were first tasked with feeding the crowd, I took note that they weren't asked to forgo their own meal to ensure the others would be well-fed. There was enough for them also. Extra, even.

Would there be for me? Could this bread in my hand be blessed to become the sufficiency I sought?

I paused to partake of that which I'd been given. "Strengthen me, Jesus," I whispered in prayer, "that I may not faint."

Friend, I don't know your days or what you find yourself in the midst of right now. I don't know the details of what lies ahead for you, how worn out you are from fixing plates for others or traveling your own dusty roads.

But what I do know is that Jesus turns to you each blessed morning, looks you in the eye, and in that tender knowing way of his, speaks your name. He holds out the bread and whispers the words, "Take. Eat. This is for you."

Dear heart, may you pause and partake.

Jesus, just as you were mindful of the five thousand, of their frames that just may faint, you are mindful of us. You know where we are, what lies ahead, and what we need. So hold us up, would you? And hold out to us the sustenance we need. Supply us, scene by unfolding scene. Sustain us this day, we pray.

PONDER

Imagine Jesus holding out the day's bread to you, speaking the words "Take. Eat." What is your response? What feelings arise?

Do you ever forgo eating, literally or figuratively? If so, why? What are the ramifications of this?

What haven't you tasted of in a very long time?

PRACTICE

Ask God to give you what is needed for the unique demands of your day. At day's end, spend time recalling what you were given, and how. Give thanks for the sustenance that sustained you.

Practice Communion with others, the giving and the receiving of the bread and cup.

PRAY

Source and Sustainer, give us each our daily bread.

19

A SATISFIED SOUL

PRAYER: Satisfy my soul.

I have a carved wooden bowl that I hold when I pray. I call it my Soul Bowl. In the mornings, I lift it up and hold it before God, offering to God the contents of my soul, pouring it all out before him. And then I wait and ask God to fill this bowl with what he knows I need.

The other day, I had to eat a lot of stress, swallowing it straight down, and I felt how it emptied me out. The next morning, as I held my bowl up to God, I chuckled as I heard myself ask for a cookie. I needed something sweet after the previous day's stress. Some comfort food, please.

Now, I have a pretty good diet. I eat my fruits and veggies and watch my sugars. I even bought one of those green powder drinks recently to get all my micronutrients in. After a childhood of eating one too many bags of barbecue potato chips, I think I'm doing pretty well right now.

And yet I wonder at how I so often neglect to eat what's good for me. I'm not talking brussels sprouts here (although, admittedly, they're not my favorite) but beauty. Why is it that I tend to only take in the bitter?

I've had long seasons of feasting on the bread of my affliction and the water of oppression (Isa. 30:20). Like the psalmist, I've had lean years where "my tears have been my food day and night" (Ps. 42:3, NIV). I can become so accustomed to this diet that I forget to feast on anything else. That is, until I realize how malnourished I've become.

Recently, on a weekend away, I changed my diet. While working on my writing, I treated myself to a cup of tea out at a cafe. Then to lunch. I took long walks around the city, admiring the architecture. I fed my hungry soul with a book club on creativity before taking it to a five o'clock Mass that satiated my senses with the stained-glass windows, the bread and the wine, and the music that swelled in my soul. I went to bed thinking, "This is what nourishment feels like," and it left me hungry for more.

"When your soul is famished and withering, He fills you with good and beautiful things, satisfying you as long as you live," the psalmist said of God (Ps. 103:5, VOICE).

"Hearken diligently to Me," God says to his people, "and eat what is good, and let your soul delight itself in fatness [the profuseness of spiritual joy]" (Isa. 55:2, AMPC).

I think *this* is the kind of weight I want to gain—to go from famished to fat because I'm feasting on joy!

God, when our plates are full of the hard, give us heapings of help, mounds of mercy, spoonfuls of that which will satisfy our souls.

PONDER

What might you be forgetting to feast on? What is missing from your diet (physically, emotionally, relationally, spiritually)?

What would feed your senses and satisfy your soul? How can you get more of it?

PRACTICE

Take yourself out on a date to engage in something that feeds your senses. This could be a walk in the woods, a long drive, a meal, an art gallery, a concert—you get the idea. Use your imagination and feast on something good.

Find a bowl to use as your Soul Bowl. As you pray, lift it up to God, pouring out your heart to him. Then ask for his filling.

PRAY

Giver of all good gifts, satisfy my soul.

SUSTAINING GRACE

PRAYER: Sustain me and see me through.

I was praying this morning for a few friends who are walking long, hard roads. I asked God to support them. I asked God to strengthen them. And then, at the end of my prayer, the word *sustain* came forth.

Sustain them, I prayed. *Give them sustaining grace. Grace for the long haul.*

Like Goldilocks trying out each of the three bears' beds, that word *sustain* seemed to fit the need just right.

Sometimes we need momentary grace—help in time of need. And sometimes, friend, we need sustaining grace. Grace that lasts. Grace that stretches over the wide expanse of desert sands. Grace that possibly holds more than helps.

"Cast your burden on the Lord [releasing the weight of it] and He will sustain you," the psalmist said (Ps. 55:22, AMPC). He will hold you up.

The use of the word *burden* in the above Scripture refers not just to the load we bear (which is how I typically think of it), but also to the lot we've been given in life. Take a deep breath and think about that for a moment.

In fact, let's try it on for size. Say it with me? "Cast your [lot in life] on the Lord—releasing the weight of it—and He will sustain you." Sigh.

Sustain, as you know, means to nourish and provide sustenance. But it also means to contain. To hold. In other words, God can hold the whole of us. Indeed, God always has.

I was reminded of this beautiful truth on the morning of my sixtieth birthday. God's gift to me came through the prophet Isaiah yet again:

"Listen to me, [Jennifer Lynn Gehman], you whom I have upheld since your birth, and have carried since you were born. Even to your old age and gray hairs, I am he, I am he who will sustain you. I have made you and I will carry you; I will sustain you and I will rescue you. I will carry you as I always have" (Isa. 46:3–4, NIV, VOICE).

God holds the whole of me, the whole way through. All the way home.

Sustaining grace, how sweet the sound, that holds the whole of me. There is no weight you cannot bear; I rest myself in thee.

PONDER

What does your lot in life feel like? Depict it using as many descriptive words as you can.

What feelings arise as you think about "releasing the weight" of the burden you bear—of your lot in life or your load? Is there any resistance?

PRACTICE

Ask someone to carry something for you this week. Pay attention to how it feels to ask and how it feels to allow them to do so.

Write your own hymn beginning with the words, "Sustaining grace, how sweet the sound . . ."

PRAY

God of all grace, sustain me and see me through.

21

CARRY OR COMPANION

PRAYER: Teach me to walk beside and not beneath.

A friend of mine was in a season of grief. She likened its weight to that of carrying an overgrown child in her arms on a long walk home. She was holding the heavy, she said, and it became heavier by the mile.

I asked her, "What if you set it down?"

I wondered how it would be for her to walk beside the grief instead of carrying it. Still present, but in a different capacity.

I'm asking myself the same question right now: "What if I set it down?"

Sometimes I forget that is even an option. Like my friend, I'm a carrier, and I'm feeling the weight of a long walk with some overly heavy things. What if I set them down? Said to the circumstance, "I can't carry you any further, but I'll companion you still."

What if I moved from beneath the burden to beside it,

from carrying to companioning, from holding up to holding with? Not to abandon but to accompany, to hold its hand rather than its heaviness? This is what I'm wondering.

We all need to walk with certain realities, and some are of significant weight. But must we live life under them? "Since God cares for you," the disciple Peter writes to the church, "let him carry all your burdens and worries" (1 Pet. 5:7, VOICE).

Because Christ carries, we can companion.

The word *burden*, as I mentioned in the previous meditation, refers to our lot in life. It's not limited to a particular problem or pain but rather encompasses the entirety of our portion (and don't we all have portions!), whatever that may be. So the invitation is to pile that portion onto God.

Since God cares, let God carry.

God, this portion we've been given is entirely too much some days, and we cannot go on carrying it. You certainly know we have tried. You know the weight of what's in our arms, so come and care; come and carry; come and companion us through.

PONDER

Who or what are you carrying, and how might you move from carrier to companion?

PRACTICE

Read the poem "Heavy" by Mary Oliver and consider the line "It's not the weight you carry but how you carry it."

PRAY

Companioning Christ, teach me to walk beside and not beneath the burdens that are mine.

22

UNDERGIRD

Prayer: Bind us together.

It feels, sometimes, like our sweet world is coming apart at the seams, like a ship in a violent storm. Pummeled by wave after battering wave, our moaning can rival that of the raging winds.

I am feeling that right now. And this morning, I asked God for a word that might hold us up and hold us together in all this breaking apart.

Undergird is the word I heard.

Undergird, I came to find out, is a nautical term that involves wrapping chains or ropes around splintering ships. Back in the day, these ships would be wrapped four to five times, over and under and over once more. Held together in the howling winds.

This word *undergird* is found only twice in the Scriptures. Once is in the depiction of a literal hurricane the apostle Paul was caught up in (Acts 27:17), and the other is in Hebrews 4:16, where it's translated as the word *help*: "Let us then approach God's throne of grace with confidence, so that we may receive mercy and find grace to *help* us [undergird us, hold us together] in our time of need" (NIV).

Today, the process of undergirding a ship is called *frapping*. A ship is frapped to support her in a great storm when she is simply not strong enough to resist the violent efforts of the sea. She is frapped to support her when she is in danger of sinking, to give her a chance to survive.

This is what I pray for us now.

As our world breaks apart under so much strain, let us approach God to be frapped in our time of need. Frapped and wrapped round and about by mercy and grace so strong it can hold us up and hold us together even in the fiercest of storms.

God who undergirds, this storm is too much, and we, your people, are in danger of breaking entirely apart. Wrap us round and about and round once more. You are our whole hope.

PONDER

What is threatening to pull you apart or pull you under? To what storm are you in danger of succumbing?

PRACTICE

Wrap yourself up in a blanket like a tamale, as if you are cocooned or swaddled. Feel the sensation of being held together.

PRAY

Undergirding God, bind us together with cords that cannot
be broken.

DO NOT DISTURB

PRAYER: Settle my soul.

I've recently been drawn to Psalm 131, in which the psalmist David described himself as God's "resting child" (v. 2, TPT). And I wonder: How might I describe myself? What adjective would I use?

In my family of origin, I was the compliant child—the fixer, the pleaser, the caretaker of sorts. But who am I now, and how am I today?

This morning, my adjective of choice was *rattled*.

I am not your resting child, I told God. *I'm your rattled one, blown hither and yon by the winds and waves that be.*

Jesus spoke to this condition once. He was in the Upper Room with his disciples, and everything was poised to change. One in their community had just left to betray him, and Peter was told he'd soon follow suit.

Not only would these friends abandon Jesus, but, Jesus told them, he would be leaving all of them. And these disciples, who had followed him round and about for three full years, would not be able to follow him where he was going next.

Jesus followed this bombshell news with the most absurd of words. "Don't let this rattle you," he said. "You trust God, don't you?" (John 14:1, MSG). To which I would have replied, "Do you want me to answer that honestly, Jesus? Because right now, I'm feeling rather shaken and stirred!"

As I sat in silence, cup of tea in hand, the words "Do not disturb" sat down with my rattling soul. And I knew they were for me and I could share them with you.

Do not disturb. We can hang these words on our front doors as a keep-out sign, as a stay-away sign, as a do-not-interrupt-my-peace sign. We can hang them as an attempt to control that which comes our way. But, alas, life is no respecter of those signs and marches its madness in anyway. Have you noticed?

So rather than this, I suggest we hang a version of these words on our hearts instead: "Do not (be) disturb(ed)." Oh, that changes everything, doesn't it?

Do not be disturbed. I hang these words not on my door to keep a thing out, but rather on my heart to keep a peace in. I hang them as a reminder that no matter the madness that marches, my center can hold.

I need not be moved, rattled, shaken, or stirred. And if and when I am—because, hello!—may these words remind me I can return. From rattled to resting once more.

God, we are your rattled children. But we are your children. Hush us, please. Gather us up. Soothe our fears and smooth our ruffled feathers. Return us to rest. Return us to you. And center us down once more.

PONDER

If you were to describe yourself this very minute, what adjective would you use?

What news rattles you?

Answer Jesus's question: "You trust God, don't you?"

PRACTICE

Learn about and begin to practice centering prayer.

Purchase a "Do Not Disturb" door hanger. Then, using a marker, change the wording to "Do Not Be Disturbed," and hang it where you need it most.

PRAY

Prince of Peace, settle my soul.

24

DROP ANCHOR

PRAYER: Be an anchor to my soul.

I live sometimes as if I have no anchor, as if I am at the mercy of the whipping winds and swelling seas. But this morning, in the inky darkness of predawn hours, a bit restless and reeling from the chaos of it all, I was reminded otherwise. As the writer of Hebrews once wrote, "We have this hope as an anchor for the soul, firm and secure" (Heb. 6:19, NIV).

We have an anchor.

Let that sink in—literally.

We have an anchor for our souls. And our anchor's name is *hope*.

It is hope in God's promises and presence that holds us. And we, in turn, are invited to hold it—"to grasp the hope that is lying in front of us" (v. 18, CEB), as if it is indeed within our reach.

I have failed at this. I've forsaken my hope as it falls through my fingers, and it's left me flailing.

But this morning, those words out of Hebrews keep swirling in my soul, sinking deeper and deeper with each go around. We have this anchor. I can feel a steadying, a staying, a stilling, a strength.

We may not be spared storms or swelling seas, but neither are we at their mercy. Hallelujah, we have an anchor that drops deep as the waters rise high. We have this anchor for our souls. Forgetting this, I can be spun silly, drifting into uncharted waters and tumultuous territories as I sympathize with the psalmist's description below:

"Relentless waves lifted the ships high in the sky, then drove them down to the depths; the sailors' courage dissolved into misery. They staggered and stumbled around like drunkards, and they had no idea what to do. In their distress, they called out to the Eternal, and He saved them from their misery" (Ps. 107:26–28, VOICE).

Relentless waves, wretched conditions, and then—then the remembering. The awakening to and awareness of the anchor that remains onboard. God's presence and God's promise, which hold us fast amidst fury and fear.

Is this how Jesus slept in the boat in the middle of all that mayhem and mess (Mark 4:38–40)? Strong, firm, and steadfast, he had an anchor for his soul.

Let the seas do what they may. You, O God, are our help and stay. In order to weather, we must tether. You are our anchor that holds.

PONDER

When have you lost hope, and why?

To what are you anchoring your soul? To what will you tether in order to weather the stormy seas that be?

PRACTICE

Try a breath prayer:

> *Inhale:* Anchor of my soul
> *Exhale:* Hold me fast

PRAY

Steadfast God, be an anchor to my soul in these swelling seas.

25

WIND WHISPERER

Prayer: Whisper to my wind.

I t had been one of those days, if you know what I mean. The kind of day that involved chaos and clamor and very little calm. At the end of the day, I carried all of it with me as I climbed into bed.

The next morning found me bringing it before God and begging for new mercies. As I sat in silence, a familiar Scripture story came to mind. The one where Jesus's friends were in a boat, the boat was in a storm, and Jesus was asleep in the stern. (See Mark 4:35–41.) This felt like an accurate portrayal of the feelings rising and falling within me.

As I became curious about this story, I saw something I hadn't seen before—a progression of sorts I had previously missed. I noticed the wind whipped the waves, the waves overwhelmed the boat, and the overwhelm caused the panic to rise.

And Jesus, when woken, walked it back to the source, the wind.

My personal go-to method in these moments is to participate in the panic by jumping in to bail the boat, all while the wind still howls and the waves whip wild. I can tell you from years of experience that this is both exhausting and ineffective, typically serving only to add to the chaos and chase away the calm.

Jesus didn't do that. He didn't begin by telling his frantic friends to calm down. Nor did he grab a bucket to help them bail. Before speaking to the worries or the waves, Jesus addressed the wind—that unseen source of the fury and the fuss.

"He [Jesus] told the wind to pipe down," Mark tells us. "And the wind ceased (sank to rest as if exhausted by its beating) and there was [immediately] a great calm (a perfect peacefulness)" (v. 39, MSG, AMPC).

Jesus was, and is, a wind whisperer. I want to be one too.

Calm me, O Lord, as you stilled the storm. Still me, O Lord, keep me from harm. Let all the tumult within me cease. Enfold me, Lord, in your peace. (Celtic Prayer)

PONDER

What is your wind, and what words help calm it?

Do you, in good-intentioned ways, create more clamor than calm?

PRACTICE

The next time panic arises in you or one close to you, try to walk it back to its source and speak to it there.

Fill a bowl with water and then slosh it about. What do you notice about the waves you create? Or how it feels to do the sloshing? Or how it would feel to be riding those waves in a tiny boat?

PRAY

Storm-settling Savior, whisper to my wind and calm the sea in me.

26

A TALE OF TWO BIRDS

PRAYER: May my presence bring peace.

It was an early spring evening when my husband brought our hanging plants inside to protect them from a dip in temperature. No sooner had he set one of the plants down when a sweet little Carolina wren shot out of it. In its confused state, it began a panicked flight through the rooms in our home.

Quite surprised ourselves, we gave chase. The wren darted this way and that, with us in hot pursuit, our son's butterfly net in hand.

After thirty minutes of flurried activity, the bird and my husband were shut into a one-windowed bedroom. The showdown intensified and ended, finally, with the bird's escape to the great outdoors.

We were tuckered out from all of the commotion and could only imagine how the poor wren felt. While we had her best interest in mind, I think our methods must have traumatized the dear thing, and I don't blame her if she went in search of a new place to nest.

Last week, a friend told me of a bird who had recently found its way into her home too. I expected a harried tale not unlike our own, but that is not what unfolded. Her bird was a finch, nesting in a wreath on her front door. When my friend opened the door to allow the breeze to flow, the finch took flight inside.

Unlike my husband and me, my friend responded by sitting still. For thirty minutes, she sat in silence. As she watched the bird fly this way and that, she didn't pursue. She didn't panic. No butterfly nets needed. As my friend sat still as stone, the finch found its own way out.

Two birds. Two houses. Two very different stories.

In this tale of two birds, the difference is this: My friend offered a non-anxious presence to her visitor. My husband and I did not. Where my friend was silent and still, we matched our little bird's anxiety and thereby likely increased it. We didn't mean to. We wanted to help. But our help likely did more harm than good.

The outcome for both birds was the same, but the means by which it came, the energy exerted, and the trauma levels experienced were vastly different.

I long to be a non-anxious presence to all who come my way. Not only to birds but people. Not only to people but thoughts, feelings, grief, or pain. Things I'd rather shoo out the door as quickly as possible. Can I be in their presence in a calm way?

My thoughts turn to the story of Jesus asleep in the boat while a storm raged (Luke 8:22–25). The disciples were incensed. How could he? Why wasn't he matching their level of distress? Didn't he care? Wake him up and make him help!

I used to side with the disciples, but I am beginning to see it differently now. Might Jesus be to us like my friend to the finch? A peaceful presence in a panicked world.

Oh peaceful Jesus, we your people get so worked up and worried while you remain calm and cool. Be near us so we can regulate our rushing to your rootedness and return to a centered spot.

PONDER

Who is a non-anxious presence for you?

What, like our little bird, has entered your life unbidden, and how might you be a non-anxious presence to it?

PRACTICE

The next time you start getting caught in the fray, take one deep breath and one step back. Pause to pray about the presence you bring to the situation.

Schedule a time to be with someone who is a non-anxious presence for you. Simply enjoy their company.

PRAY

Calming Christ, may my presence bring peace.

A HANDOUT OF WHOLENESS

Prayer: Hand me your wholeness.

I f you could write your own job description, what might it contain? What would you love to do that fits who you are and what you bring? What would you deem to be an absolute delight of a way to spend your day?

I wondered this as I ran across one of God's job descriptions recently while reading the book of Haggai. Speaking of what he'd do in the temple that was then being built, God said, "I will hand out wholeness" (Hag 2:9, MSG).

Hand out wholeness. Yes, this seems to be what God does from wherever God dwells.

I picture Jesus when he walked among us, handing out wholeness each day as he fed the hungry, blessed the children, touched the lepers, and defended the destitute. Offering forgiveness and hope, healing and help is what he did from where he dwelt.

God continues the work of handing out wholeness to this very day, but it's now we who are the temple from which he sets up shop. "You realize, don't you, that you are the temple of God, and God himself is present in you?" Paul asks (1 Cor. 3:16, MSG).

We are the place God's spirit dwells. Which means we are the place from which God now does that which God does: hands out wholeness.

I think of Jesus's disciples who were stopped by a lame man begging for money. "I don't have a nickel to my name," Peter told him, "but what I do have, I give you: In the name of Jesus Christ of Nazareth, walk!" (Acts 3:6, MSG). And the lame man leapt! Peter and John handed out wholeness.

It's the work of the Spirit of God and the work of the church and the work of our hands each day.

"Let's walk right up to him [God] and get what he is so ready to give," the writer of Hebrews encourages us. "Take the mercy, accept the help, an appropriate blessing, coming just at the right moment" (Heb. 4:16, MSG, AMPC).

God's great gifts—handouts of wholeness for all.

God, we're coming to your house, knocking on your door with our begging bowls in hand. We need a handout and hand up. You are the giver of all good gifts. Give us what makes us whole.

PONDER

If your job description was to hand out wholeness, how might that reframe what you do or how you do it?

Who has handed wholeness to you?

PRACTICE

Volunteer for or donate to an organization that works toward greater harmony, healing, or hope in our world.

Each day this week, give something of yourself (time, talents, or treasures) to another for their well-being.

PRAY

Generous God, hand me your wholeness.

RISKY BEHAVIOR

PRAYER: May I cast forth all I carry.

God and I were talking about sowing seeds the other day. I was suggesting we sow them one by one, in a meticulous, metered, and measured way. And preferably in the controlled environment of a greenhouse, please. Secured, safe, and sound.

God had a different plan.

I'd like to think my careful, cautious—and okay, somewhat controlling—way of approaching my work is simply being responsible and faithful with what I've been given. But God's risky plan unearthed some other possibilities.

Like the possibility that my cautious ways may be tied more to a fear of failure than to faithfulness. Ouch.

"Scatter them," God said, concerning those seeds. As in, "Once there was a sower who scattered seeds." (See Matthew 13:3.)

I was appalled. Such risky and reckless behavior! Where

will the seeds land? How will they be? What will happen to them?

Did you know that in the parable of the sower, the scattered seed failed in three out of the four places it fell?

- The path, where the seeds were eaten by birds.
- The rocky places, where the roots couldn't form.
- The thorns, which crowded and choked those poor little plants.

I don't find this to be such a good track record. That sower should be more careful, I thought. What a waste of seed! Must build a greenhouse.

Caution is defined as care taken to avoid danger or mistakes. The phrase "care taken to avoid" stands out to me. It's a descriptor of me but certainly not of God.

No, God is not cautious. And God is definitely not metered or measured. And if God were worried about failure, he certainly wouldn't have chosen the people he did throughout history to bear his name or carry out his work.

When I read the parable of the sower in the past, my focus was on what kind of soil I was and how I received the seed. It has now shifted to ponder what kind of sower I am and how I release my seeds.

"Remember what is written about the One who trusts in the Lord: He scattered abroad" (2 Cor. 9:9, VOICE).

God, we so often desire safe places with sure outcomes before sowing our seed, but that's not how it works, neither in the farm fields nor your kingdom. Help us to trust and be unafraid. Give us both the seed to sow and the courage to throw it—and our caution—to the wind.

PONDER

What kind of sower are you?

What, if anything, prevents you from casting forth the seeds you carry?

PRACTICE

Try something new. Take a risk. Journal about how it went for you.

PRAY

Risk-taking God, help me to cast forth all I carry in confidence and hope.

ROLL AND REPOSE

PRAYER: I rest myself within your care.

As hubby and I prepared to go to Europe, I felt anxious about our trip. We would be gone almost a month, which we'd never done before.

I worried about the weather and if it would be too warm for me. I wondered if I'd get any sleep, due to the six-hour time change and all the different beds in which we'd lay our heads. I felt apprehensive about the new foods I'd eat and how my digestive system would receive them. I held concern over things here on the home front, with friends, family, and the work I'd be leaving behind. And with the variety of trains, planes, and automobiles we'd be traveling on—including the German autobahn!—I worried about our safety.

Jenny, Jenny, I heard God saying over me, just as Jesus said to Martha, *you worry about so many things.* (See Luke 10:41.)

As we prepared, I was intrigued by a set of "R" words that

emerged, eager to companion me along the way: *roll and repose.*

"Commit your way to the Lord," the psalmist penned. "[*Roll and repose* each care of your load on Him]" (Ps. 37:5, emphasis added, AMPC).

To *roll* is to cause something to move somewhere else by turning it over and over. And *repose* is a state of resting or lying down and letting be. To roll and repose each load of our care (*each* load, friend!) is to move those cares over to God and then—and this can be the tricky part for some of us—let them rest there.

As I pictured this process, I saw myself rolling what looked to be a large, ancient boulder of a burden up the side of the mountain. It wasn't smooth going. The stone was heavy and awkward. The mountain path, rocky. My footsteps, faltering.

When I finally reached the place of release, I stood there, hand on this heavy burden. It was time for the letting go. Time to leave it there. Time to allow it, and me, to rest. To repose.

Honestly, I'm not sure which was harder, the rolling or reposing. That release takes a great deal of trust.

In the end, our trip was a dream come true. Everyone and everything on the home front was fine. All the travel was smooth. I slept better there than at home, navigated the weather, and enjoyed the food. Our needs were more than cared for by a plethora of generous friends and a few kindhearted strangers—*and* I broke no bones when I fell off my e-bike (a story for another time!).

God, we're sometimes crushed by the burdens we bear. We roll them to you to leave in your care.

PONDER

Describe the shape, weight, and makeup of the burdens you desire to roll on over to God. What does the path look like between here and there?

As you stand with your hand on those burdens you've just listed, what do you want to say to God about them? What might God say to you?

Which do you find more difficult, the rolling or reposing? Why?

PRACTICE

Find some Play-Doh or clay. Each morning, roll it into a ball and tell God about a burden you bear. Then place the ball down, roll it to a new place, and leave it there for the day.

PRAY

God of the burdens that I bear, I rest myself within your care.

SPARED, SAVED, OR STRENGTHENED

PRAYER: Spare me! Save me!

I want to be spared or saved, not strengthened. This is what I said to God recently, and I meant it. I realize, however, that while several people in the Scriptures were saved out of their circumstances—Daniel in the lion's den comes to mind—it is not the overarching story. Neither, sadly, has it been mine. It wasn't even that of Jesus.

As he faced his own death, Jesus prayed, "Father, if you are willing, remove this cup from Me; yet not My will, but [always] yours be done. And there appeared to Him an angel from heaven, strengthening Him in spirit" (Luke 22:42–43, AMPC).

However miraculous the strengthening by this one lone angel was, it was most likely not Jesus's desired outcome. In the garden, full of grief, Jesus didn't want what lay before him, and he named it out loud. (Can we recognize the courage it takes to do so?) "Remove this," Jesus pleaded. "Take this away from me. Spare me. Save me." But alas, even he was strengthened instead.

Just a few days prior, Jesus was paraded through thick throngs, riding on a donkey. With palm branches waving in hands held high, the crowds cried, "Hosanna! Save us! Spare us this suffering!" It causes me to wonder if, as Jesus knelt alone in the garden, the cries of that crowd still rang in his ears. If his words echoed theirs, his humanity joining hands with theirs.

This is what I want to say to you: Jesus knows what it's like to be strengthened instead of spared.

I also want to say it is okay to not want to drink the cup that is before you.

Friend, it is okay to not want to drink the cup that is before you. You are in good company here, companioned by the likes of Jesus and also the apostle Paul—a leader of the church who asked God three times to remove his pain but instead received the power to bear it (2 Cor. 12:7–10).

I pray you be spared from the pain and the problems. I truly do. I pray you be saved out of them. But if, dear one, you are not, I pray your sweet soul will be strengthened in and through it to the very, very end.

God, I ask that you would accompany and attend to us in any and every reality that is not yet removed. Amen and amen.

PONDER

What is your reality that has not (yet) been removed? What would you like to say to Jesus about it?

How do you react to being strengthened instead of spared or saved out of your suffering?

PRACTICE

Write a prayer of lament. Lament psalms follow a typical pattern:

> *Protest:* Tell God what is wrong.
> *Petition:* Tell God what you want him to do about it.
> *Praise:* Express trust based on God's character.

(For some examples, take a look at Psalms 6, 10, 13, 17, 22, 25, 31, 69, 73, 86, 88, 102.)

PRAY

Spare me! Save me! Or strengthen me, I pray.

HOST WITHOUT HOLDING

PRAYER: *Help me to receive all that comes.*

I've been thinking a lot about space this year. How to create space. How to hold space. How to take up space. And now, how to offer space.

I find that offering space is very different than, say, offering help. It's, well, spacious. It's non-manipulative and without agenda. Offering space invites but doesn't control.

The trees I love so much are schooling me in how to do this well.

I watch as a tree offers space to scampering squirrels that run up and down its length. To woodpeckers that carve it out and to children who climb its branches. To both delightful chickadees and demanding crows (sometimes simultaneously). To the rains, winds, and sun.

All of it is allowed by the tree. All received. None refused. The tree doesn't demand that they come, nor that they remain, nor that they leave. There is complete freedom. A tree may host, but it does not hold.

Did you know that a host is defined as a person who receives? To receive all that comes. To grant it access and take it in.

The apostle Paul spoke of this in his letter to the Romans when he said, "Welcome and receive [to your hearts] one another, then, even as Christ has welcomed and received you, for the glory of God" (Rom. 15:7, AMPC).

I find this openhanded hosting—this offering of space for both the coming and the going—to be helpful, health-full, and healing in my own life. Not only in relation to people, but also to emotions and events that come my way. No guarding, no gripping, all grace.

To open and offer space in such a way as to host all of life and all it brings is an exercise in abiding trust and a precious gift to give.

May we be able to receive and release while remaining deeply rooted. May we allow all of life and all it holds to both come and go. May we not close, not clamp, not clutch, not control. Grace us, O God, we pray.

PONDER

What does the tree of your life currently host? What people, emotions, or situations?

What feelings rise up as you think about receiving each one and giving them space? Allowing them to both come and go?

PRACTICE

Draw a picture of your life's tree that includes all that you
host. Consider drawing the people, emotions, or events as
animals (birds, squirrels, bears, monkeys, etc.). Notice what's
there and even how they interact with each other. Notice
what's missing.

PRAY

Welcoming God, help me to receive all that comes.

BE FREE

PRAYER: Set me free.

I t was the end of a difficult year and I was in a worship service, trying to focus on God and whatever good I could find.

Just then, someone through whom my family had experienced harm walked into the service and sat opposite me. I felt my body begin to shut down.

And then the Spirit whispered words that opened me back up: "Be free! Be free! It's the year of Jubilee!"

The year of Jubilee, I knew, was a God-ordained time and season when all debts were released. I recognized Spirit's words as an invitation to make a choice. I could continue to carry this pain into the new year, or I could release it and let it go.

In Matthew 18, Jesus demonstrates the power of forgiveness by telling a story about a servant who was released from his debt. Greatly relieved, the servant then searched for someone indebted to him. One might think he did so in order to respond in kind, but no. Instead of passing on the grace he received, he grabbed this indebted one, tightened his grip around the man's neck, and demanded he pay back what he owed.

I don't want to be like this man. There is another way. Be free! Be free! It's the year of Jubilee.

I find myself repeating Spirit's mantra now as soon as an offense occurs. When others don't do what I want or give what I need. When words or actions (or lack thereof) cause pain: "Be free! Be free! It's the year of Jubilee!"

You might think it's them I'm speaking to, them I'm releasing. And maybe in part, you'd be right. But the truth of the matter is, I'm freeing myself: "Be free! Be free! It's the year of Jubilee!"

God whose forgiveness is deep and wide, set us free. Grant us the grace to live with abandon and lightness, and root us in a love so deep that letting go becomes possible.

PONDER

What people or pain are you continuing to carry? What could it be like to set them free?

What do you feel you are owed, and by whom? It might be money or a long-borrowed tool, but more likely it's time, an apology, honor, respect, recognition, the truth.

PRACTICE

Pay attention to when you feel irritated or offended by

someone. (This may include God, life in general, and even your own body.) Ask yourself, "What do I feel they owe me that I'm not getting?" Shake your hands and say out loud, "Be free! Be free! It's the year of Jubilee!" Repeat as many times as needed.

PRAY

God of jubilee, set me free.

FOSTER THE FLOURISHING

PRAYER: Foster my flourishing.

J esus told a story about a tree one time. A tree that wasn't doing so well. A tree that was three years in but stood buck naked amongst a backdrop of prolific producers.

The owner of the vineyard had had enough, Jesus said. "Cut it down!" the owner ordered the gardener. But instead of cutting, the gardener countered: "'Sir,' the man replied, 'leave it alone for one more year, and I'll dig around it and fertilize it'" (Luke 13:8, NIV).

And with that, the gardener set to work.

We don't know the outcome, but here's what we do know: It is possible to foster the flourishing of that which is faltering or failing.

I was thinking about this as I read Psalm 92 recently.

"The righteous will flourish like a palm tree," it reads. "They will grow like a cedar of Lebanon; planted in the house of the LORD, they will flourish in the courts of our

God. They will still bear fruit in old age, they will stay fresh and green" (vv. 12–14, NIV).

The Amplified Bible expounds on the word *flourish* with these beautiful descriptors: "They shall be full of sap [of spiritual vitality] and [rich in the] verdure [of trust, love, and contentment]" (v. 14, AMPC).

Rich in the verdure—what does that even mean?

As I came to find out, verdure is lush, green vegetation and is described as—are you ready?—a flourishing condition.

So I ask: Do trust, love, and contentment foster flourishing? Might they be the fertilizer our faltering fig tree needs? I'm going out on a limb to say yes, yes, they do, and yes, yes, they are.

Contentment is the one that gets me the most. The one in which I lack. This word means a permanent habit of trusting in God's goodness. That bears repeating: *a permanent habit*—in the face of all the things—of trusting in God's goodness. I cannot imagine a more flourishing condition than that.

"I have learned how to be content," the apostle Paul wrote, "(satisfied to the point where I am not disturbed or disquieted) in whatever state I am in" (Phil. 4:11, AMPC). Not disturbed or disquieted? Sounds like flourishing to me.

God, bring us to this flourishing state, rich in the verdure of love, trust, and contentment, that all good things may grow from there.

PONDER

What, if anything, around you or within you is faltering, failing, or in need of a little fertilizer?

What do you most need to have spread at the base of your soul—love, trust, or contentment?

PRACTICE

Consider one action you can take, large or small, to foster the flourishing of your family, community, church, town, or workplace. Take that action this week.

Give your plants (indoor or out) a treat. Buy some fertilizer as food for their flourishing.

PRAY

Foster my flourishing, Gardener God.

34

THE TREE OF Z

PRAYER: I want to be like a tree.

I've long loved being tucked under trees. Having spent my childhood years camping, trees have always felt like home to me. To this day, wandering in the woods brings all my hurried insides into a holy hush. Trees center me, as if their deep roots call out to my own.

I am more fascinated by trees than ever before. By how they thrive in community, share nutrients with one another, and watch each other's backs (or should I say bark?). I'm finding that the trees I've grown to love so much are resourceful, generous, and generative, fostering life for a full century after they've fallen. Yes, I want to be like a tree.

I believe God wants me to be like a tree as well. And according to Scripture, there are quite a few options.

I could be like the tree planted by streams of water or like the green olive tree in the house of God (Ps. 1:3; 52:8). I could flourish like the palm tree or grow like a cedar in Lebanon (Ps. 92:12). Being an oak of righteousness might be nice (Isa. 61:3). Or how about the tree that has no fear when heat comes and never ceases to bear fruit (Jer. 17:8)? Yes, please, to any of these trees.

But at this very moment in time? The tree I would really like to be is the tree that helped Zacchaeus see.

In the story of Zacchaeus, we find a man rich in wealth, short in stature, and stealing from those in town. He was a despised man, a dishonest man, and a man whose desire to see Jesus drove him to climb a tree. A sycamore, to be exact.

Luke tells us Zacchaeus was "trying to see who Jesus was" (Luke 19:3, NRSV). But his seeing was impeded by his height and the crowd. So in order to see, he climbed a tree. That's the tree I want to be. A tree that helps people to see. One I will now call "the tree of Z."

Zacchaeus climbed his tree to see who Jesus was, but I think he got more than he bargained for. For not only did Zacchaeus see Jesus, but he saw Jesus seeing him in return.

And it didn't stop there. From his place perched in that tree, Zacchaeus received and responded to an invitation from Jesus. The result was life trickling out, life trickling down, life flowing all over that surprised little town.

God, may we be like this tree. To have low-lying branches, accessible to all, trees for which others don't have to be tall. Trees who hold others above all the crowds. Trees that help quiet all that is loud. Trees who do not judge those who come; trees who welcome an unholy one. A place folks can come to find and be found; a place where they can both hear and respond.

PONDER

Who has served as a "tree of Z" to you?

What kind of tree do you want to be, and why?

What do you notice the tree in this story doing—or perhaps more importantly, not doing?

PRACTICE

Climb a tree . . . but please be careful!

Engage in imaginative prayer. Put yourself in the role of Zacchaeus. Pay attention to how it feels not only to see Jesus but to see Jesus seeing you. What invitation does Jesus offer? How do you respond?

PRAY

God of me, I want to be like a tree.

35

HOPEFUL LIVING

PRAYER: Grant me your words of life.

Photos of my ancestors line the walls of my home. I long for their presence here, for their lives to live on and to inform mine.

There are my grandparents who traveled the globe via freight boats and a VW bus. My great-grandmother who, alongside her husband, swung the doors of heart and home wide as she championed women's rights and education in Japan. Her sister, who penned poems through her pain. And their father, who, as a widower, took his young daughters on world tours, ensuring they learned the language wherever they roamed.

And then there's my favorite: my tenth great-grandfather, Paul Gerhardt, a pastor in the 1600s who is known to this day as Germany's most beloved hymn writer. A man who faced deep suffering with an even deeper faith.

These are formidable days we are living in. Unprecedented, some say. I believe we can take courage, gain wisdom, and find our way forward by following patterns and paths of the past.

As the wise King Solomon once prayed, "May [God] keep us centered and devoted to Him, following the life path He has cleared, watching the signposts, walking at the pace and rhythms he laid down for our ancestors" (1 Kings 8:57–58, MSG).

The prophet Jeremiah echoed the wisdom of those words when he encouraged his people, "Stand at the crossroads and look; ask for the ancient paths, ask where the good way is, and walk in it" (Jer. 6:16, NIV).

Follow the path. Watch for the signposts. Walk at the pace that's been set. Stand at the crossroads. Survey the surroundings. Seek before setting out. What important spiritual practices these are as we live out our days.

What guidance can you glean from those who have gone before? Some questions I like to ask as I look at my ancestors' lives are:

- What did you do with your grief?
- Where did you go for guidance?
- How did you hold on to hope?
- What might you long for me to learn from your life?

If you don't know the stories of your ancestors, read biographies of others or steep in some of the Scripture stories, asking those characters the same questions as above.

As Paul wrote in Romans 15:4, "Everything written in the days of old was recorded to give us instructions for living. We find encouragement through the Scriptures and a call to perseverance that will produce hopeful living" (VOICE).

Hopeful living. That sounds like a rare commodity these

days. May we find our way forward by following a path that was laid out long before.

Rock of Ages, forever faithful, guide us in the well-worn ways of love.

PONDER

What do you want future generations to glean from your life? How can you live into that now?

Who is one of your favorite ancestors, and why? What questions would you like to ask him or her?

PRACTICE

Research your family tree. Learn a new story or two about those in your past.

Intentionally spend time with an older person, asking some of the questions posed above.

Write a letter to someone in a future generation, offering your own wisdom and stories. What hope might you hold out to them?

PRAY

Ancient of Days, grant me your words of life.

36

CREATE EMPTY

Prayer: Full-fill me.

I've had a harrowing relationship with hope. While I believe we can't live without it, there have been long stretches where attempting to live with it has felt achingly impossible.

In Romans 5, Paul talks about hope as something that ultimately rises out of our suffering. According to him, suffering produces endurance, which produces character, which produces, you guessed it, hope.

I have a feeling this equation is like one of those interminable math problems in my college statistics class. You eventually get to the bottom of it, but it's a lot more complicated than two plus two.

However long it takes us to get there, Paul says, this hope that awaits us does not disappoint.

In The Message, Eugene Petersen put it this way: "In alert expectancy [hope] such as this, we're never left feeling short changed. Quite the contrary—we can't round up enough containers to hold everything God generously pours into our lives through the Holy Spirit!" (v. 5).

Waiting expectantly for God to fill the empty spaces is a habit of hope. It reminds me of the story in 2 Kings 4 of a widow who had been emptied—emptied of her husband, her possessions and provisions, and very soon her two sons, set to be sold as slaves.

Destitute, this woman cried out to the prophet Elisha, who offered what appeared to be irrational advice. Learning this woman had nothing of value in her home but a tiny bit of olive oil, Elisha said, "Go outside, borrow vessels from all your neighbors, empty vessels and not just a few" (v. 3, NRSV).

Empty, the prophet said, and not just a few. Ridiculous! How about instructing this poor woman to ask her neighbors for full jars? And while she's at it, for bread, spare change, and a job or two for her and her boys? Elisha's advice seems overwhelmingly unhelpful.

When the widow came to her neighbors, I'd like to believe that along with those empty jars, they lent her their hope. I'd like to think they gave their belief. That along with the jars, they held out holy anticipation and expectation. That they were with her in the wonder and the waiting.

A habit of hope is not only harrowing. It can be downright hard. What if all this empty isn't filled?

And yet the invitation remains: to stand, day after day, at the corner of emptiness and expectancy. Perhaps we'll meet there, you and I, and together hold our empty high in this daily habit of hope.

God, we come. Empty and expectant, terrified and trusting, looking to you. Fill us with your Holy Spirit and with your hope, we pray.

PONDER

In what seasons has it been hard for you to hope?

What do you do with your empty? Are there any unhelpful ways you attempt to fill it?

How might you create *more* empty in anticipation of God's filling?

What "neighbors" can you invite to participate in this process of hope with you?

PRACTICE

Create empty by engaging in some silence and solitude, fasting a meal, turning off the TV, or cleaning out your closet.

Sit with your empty (unfulfilled hopes, grief, or losses). Feel the weight of it. Invite God, who hovered over the empty and void (Gen. 1:2), to be in it with you.

PRAY

God of green hope, full-fill me.

STUMP SPROUT

PRAYER: Cause this stump to sprout once more.

T his year, I've been paying close attention to trees. I am leaning in, listening, and seeking to learn from them.

As I do, the words of Job—a man whose life had been chopped down, limb by limb—have been a gift and grace to me.

"For a tree there is always hope," he said. "Chop it down and it still has a chance—its roots can put out fresh sprouts. Even if its roots are old and gnarled, its stump long dormant, at the first whiff of water it comes to life, buds and grows like a sapling" (Job 14:7–9, MSG).

"There is always hope," said this grieving man. "Chop [the tree] down and it still has a chance."

There's a phenomenon in the natural world called stump sprouting. I wonder if this is what Job was referencing. New life rising from the old.

On the eve of my sixtieth birthday, the image of a tree

came to mind as I thought about how I wanted to mark that threshold. I thought about how the "tree of me" has known some axe blows in its time and has withstood many storms. I wondered: Might it (or I?) receive a blessing to strengthen and sprout once more?

Knowing that trees thrive in community, I called upon mine.

I decided to commission an artist friend to paint a tree for me, and I invited loved ones to contribute their words. I asked for blessings to be written all over the roots, trunk, and branches of the painting to serve as sources of sap, strength, and support. I asked for words of affirmation to be writ on the leaves, a testament to the fruit of my life thus far.

That painting now hangs above my desk. A tree in community with others that has sprouted from a stump, risen from the remains, and serves as a reminder to open and offer in the years yet to come.

Hope can be hard to come by sometimes. Job felt that full on. In fact, if you read one verse further in the passage, you will notice he didn't hold the same hope for humans that he did for trees.

Imagine his surprise, then, when new life sprouted, even for him.

From that which has been cut off or cut down, life can emerge once more—life that is fed by that which was felled, by that which was former. There remains seed and substance in the stump, and a sprout may yet come forth.

Bless us, O God, with hope, with brave little shoots that dare to sprout and bear life once more.

PONDER

What is it like for you to consider that what has been chopped down still has a chance? That from the stump, new life might sprout?

PRACTICE

Go for a walk—in the woods, especially, if there's one nearby —and look for stump sprouts. When you find one, pray for its well-being and yours.

PRAY

God of new life, cause this stump to sprout once more.

38

THE SOWER, THE SEED, AND THE SOIL

PRAYER: Make of me good soil for seeding.

I am not the sower, planting, but the soil, receiving. This is the truth that rose up in me as I once again read the parable of the sower, found in Matthew 13.

In this story Jesus spun, we are not tending, watering, weeding, or seeding. We are simply the ground opening, made ready to receive that which comes to us.

We are its host and its home.

It is costly, this becoming and being good soil, and I haven't always thrilled at the price. The truth is, the seeds are planted into the compost of my life. Tucked right down into the soil of my soul, made rich from the rending.

A wide clearing has been made in me over the years. The soil, watered by my weeping, has been enriched by all that disintegrated and dissolved before my very eyes. The composting of my previous life. Because of the breaking apart, and not in spite of it, I am a prepared place for the plantings of the Lord. And the Lord is a very good gardener:

"For the Lord will comfort Zion; he will comfort all her waste places, and will make her wilderness like Eden, her desert like the garden of the Lord; joy and gladness will be found in her, thanksgiving and the voice of song" (Isa. 51:3, NRSV).

Eugene Peterson puts it this way in The Message: "I'll transform her dead ground into Eden."

Yes and amen. That is what comfort looks like: little green bits planted in a land widened by our weeping.

Sometimes we are the seed, planted by God in specific places to take root, grow, and bear much fruit. Sometimes we are the sower, planting seeds of love, hope, generosity, and truth in the lives of others. I have been both. I am both.

But I am also the soil. Host and home to that which the Holy One hopes to grow. I am not the product or the plant that emerges from my depths. I am the depths themselves, the ground from which they grow.

The writer of Hebrews gives a hopeful word: "Ground that drinks up the rain falling on it repeatedly, and that produces a crop useful to those for whom it is cultivated, receives a blessing from God" (Heb. 6:7, NRSV).

Drink up, dear reader. Drink deep. Everything that falls can foster the flourishing. We are the seed. We are the sowers. We are the soil from which the sprouts grow.

It is hard to open when the rains are falling, God. We want to cover and cower and close. Help us to open in trust that we will not be ruined but rather restored. Or at the very least, that new life will rise from our ruins.

PONDER

How has your soul's soil been made rich by the rending, widened by the weeping?

What might be planted in the compost of your life? What do you desire?

PRACTICE

Start composting.

The next time it rains, go outside, open your arms, and lift your head to receive it in full. Then come in, dry off, and make yourself a pot of tea!

PRAY

Gardener God, make of me good soil for seeding.

39

POSTURES THAT PREPARE US

PRAYER: Posture me in preparation.

My husband and I recently flew from Pennsylvania to Colorado. Our round-trip flight meant we experienced two departures and two arrivals. Two ascents and two descents, for a total of four times hearing the flight attendant's voice over the loud-speaker instructing us to please assume our upright positions.

This got me thinking about postures that prepare us for what is to come. I began wondering if the airline instructions stood in sharp contrast to those Jesus might have received for his round-trip journey to Earth. Had he come in his full, upright position as King of Kings and Lord of Lords, he never would have fit. Earth cannot hold him.

To prepare for his arrival, Jesus had to assume not an upright position but a bent one. And bend he did, into the tiniest of seeds in a woman's dark womb.

When the time came for his departure, Jesus bent yet

again. He bent low to the ground—into the shape not of seed but servant—and washed his disciples' feet in an act of love.

We serve an upright God who is bent on bending. Bent on loving us. And who has a bent for the bent ones. A bent for the burdened ones. A bent for the ones brought low.

In the Gospels, we encounter Jesus physically bending to the ground to protect a woman caught in adultery from the upright ones about to cast stones (John 8:2–11).

We hear him defend a prostitute, bent on washing his feet with her tears (Luke 7:36–50).

We watch in wonder as he bends rigid rules and on the Sabbath heals a woman who had been physically bent for eighteen long years (Luke 13:10–17).

We marvel with the multitudes on that momentous day when Jesus blessed the bent—the meek and the mourning, the merciful ones, the persecuted, pure, and poor (Matt. 5:1–12).

I don't know what has bent you, friend—poverty, pressure, or pain. I don't know your journey, past or present, that has laid you low. But what I do know, and what I have experienced, is that our precarious bent position is the very posture that prepares us both for the arrival of God to us and our departure back to God.

It's not the rigid or right but the bent and bowed who are blessed.

An upright position may be preferred for a plane, train, or automobile. But in our walkabout daily lives, a bent frame may serve us best.

Forgive us, O God, for all our rigid rightness. Guide us into the postures that prepare us for what and who is to come.

PONDER

How do you prefer to posture yourself?

What has bent you, and how might this serve to prepare or protect you for what or who is to come?

PRACTICE

Do toe-touches each morning. Practice bending. Posture yourself before entering your day.

PRAY

Bending One, posture me in preparation for all that is to come.

40

FLOWER POWER

PRAYER: *Help me repay the bad with a blessing.*

The political climate was tense, and recent conflicts and conversations left me feeling rather disgruntled. As I poured this out in prayer, I sensed Jesus wordlessly extend a single flower my way. This simple act silenced me, and I watched in wonder as all my defenses fell. The power of a single flower.

"Flower power" was the slogan of the 1960s and stems (pardon the pun!) from the peaceful resistance to the Vietnam War. Protestors, armed with flowers, would hand them out to the opposition in hopes of reducing the level of fear, anger, and threat that existed.

As I took my own proverbial flower from the hand of Jesus, I took the message as well: *Jenny, dear one, choose peace in your response to the other. In response to the hard or the harsh you received.*

And it left me questioning: What do I extend to others? Fist or flower?

Jesus holding out the flower to me had a de-escalating effect. It offered me a different way: The way of love. The way where I don't strike back. The way where I not only hold my tongue but hold out kindness.

The disciple Peter, whose initial approach to opposition was a sword (John 18:10), later wrote, "Do not repay evil with evil or insult with insult. On the contrary, repay evil with blessing, because to this you were called so that you may inherit a blessing" (1 Pet. 3:9, NIV). Or, as the Voice translation words it, "repaying the bad with a blessing."

Flower power. Instead of responding in kind, may we respond in kind*ness*.

Jesus, your ways are life and health and peace. And your ways are challenging to follow. The Scripture is true that your ways are not our ways. We feel that, especially here. Help us to bend and help us to bless. Help us to value peace more than protection, repair more than retribution. Lead us in the ways of love.

PONDER

What is your response to the opposing side—fist or flower?

What is one small thing you can do to reduce the very real levels of fear, anger, and threat in our world today?

PRACTICE

Bless someone with whom you may disagree. Perhaps a flower or two?

PRAY

Help me, God, to repay the bad with a blessing.

41

OPENHANDED

PRAYER: Open my hands.

"You open your hand," the psalmist said of God, "and satisfy the desires of every living thing" (Ps. 145:16, NIV). This little verse, along with many others throughout the Scriptures, serves to remind me that we serve an openhanded God. This stands in contrast to how many of us too often picture God as stingy or unkind, not willing or withholding.

God is challenging my beliefs around this right now. I often have a word of the year that I live into and listen for, and this year is no exception. However, this year I've also been given a phrase. One I've been hearing off the lips of God on the daily.

"All will be given," God says, as he takes me by the hand and leads me deeper into trust—trust that I will be given what I need at the proper time from a God who withholds no good thing (Ps. 84:11).

We don't always think kindly of God's openhandedness.

It's great when it's directed toward us—don't get me wrong. But when God's lavish ways fall on those we deem undeserving, it's a whole other thing. Consider the elder brother in the parable of the prodigal son (Luke 15:11–32). God's open hand can sometimes clash with our tight fist.

"Freely you have received," Jesus said, "freely give" (Matt. 10:8, NIV). But we'd prefer to have control over to whom that giving goes.

Do we really want a God with open hands if he blesses our enemies, provides for those we deem unworthy, and rains on the just and unjust alike? And if he audaciously asks us to do the same? When faced with those who have hurt or harmed me, I'd rather remain tightfisted, thank you.

And then I'm reminded of another parable Jesus told, this one found in Matthew 18. In this story we encounter a man who had his large debt forgiven by an openhanded master, only to turn around and with two tight fists demand a friend with a lesser debt pay him back in full. It did not turn out well for this man.

We are not the judge or jury, just the ones with open hands.

God, you are good in ways we are not. Help us to believe in your generosity toward us and then to release it out to others. Open our hands to receive and to give.

PONDER

Is your experience of God one in which he has an open hand or a tight fist? Why do you think that is?

When have you witnessed God's open hand toward someone you disapprove of or count unworthy? How did that make you feel?

Have you ever experienced the kindness or generosity of God or another when you deemed yourself unworthy of it? What was that like for you?

PRACTICE

Clench your fists as tightly as you can for ten seconds, then release. Do it again. Now one more time.

In the future, when you find yourself being tightfisted in thought, feeling, or emotion, clench your hands as you did above, then open them once more.

Engage in an act of generosity toward someone who cannot pay you back in kind.

PRAY

Withholder of no good thing, open my hands.

42

STORYTIME

PRAYER: Tell me a story.

Whuse I was little, my mama told me bedtime stories spun around any three nouns I could name.

A bear, a mailbox, and a lemonade. A tent, a shoe, and a piece of string. A clown, a toothbrush, and a babydoll. You get the idea.

No matter the words I chose, Mom wove them into a story that soothed, and off to sleep I'd go.

You may not have grown up with this practice. You may even think you're incapable of weaving words in this way. But the truth of it is, most of us engage in story spinning in one form or another most days of our lives.

Think about it. We take bits and pieces of information, of situations and circumstances, of glances or gossip. Then, known to us or not, we spin a narrative around them. We connect the dots in a too-often-distorted fashion and then go about convincing ourselves of its truth.

However, these stories we spin rarely soothe. They are

often as false as my sweet mama's fiction and as tall as the tales she'd tell.

We see this in the Scriptures too. Simon the Pharisee once invited Jesus to dinner, and I say good on him for doing so! However, when a woman of "ill repute" showed up and began to wash Jesus's feet with the tears she wept, Simon was shocked and his three-word story ensued: *harlot, outcast, the talk of the town.*

Jesus didn't bite. Instead of letting Simon continue his negative narrative, Jesus interrupted him midstream. "Simon, I have something to tell you," he said.

Then he wove words of a different kind, throwing down his own set of nouns: *devoted, loved, forgiven, and freed.* The story restarted from there, the dots connecting in a more redemptive way. (See Luke 7:36–50.)

This makes me wonder if we might challenge our own spun stories. The ones we've believed about ourselves or tell about others on the daily. Might we be open to the Holy Spirit stopping us midstream by throwing down a few new nouns? Are we willing to pick up what he's putting down?

My mama told stories to lull me to sleep. But I find Jesus weaves words that wake me up wide.

Jesus, we spin so many stories about ourselves and our circumstances and those we encounter along the way. Challenge our narratives with the words you weave.

PONDER

Name your narratives. What stories do you spin:

- About your past, present, or future?
- About people (yourself included)?
- About situations or circumstances?

PRACTICE

Ask Jesus to tell you a story about _____ (fill in the blank). Maybe give him three real-life nouns: a person, a place, and a thing.

The next time you find yourself stuck in a negative narrative, ask Jesus to interrupt you with a story of his own. Be open to having your assumptions challenged.

Hold a storytelling night where you spin stories in the way my sweet mama did.

Go to a public place to engage in some people watching. Make up stories about their lives.

PRAY

Dear Jesus, tell me a better, truer story.

43

CANOPY OF KINDNESS

PRAYER: Cover me with kindness.

I prayed for kindness this week. Prayed it would be extended to those I love. That it would be stretched straight out over friend and family to provide a safe refuge in the storms that raged. Because oh, dear reader, they were raging fierce.

In Psalm 5, I notice King David doing the same as me. He's in distress, and we find him sorrowing, sighing, and seeking relief. In the midst of it all, he turns his attention to pray for those who, alongside him, seek refuge in God, and here's where I notice his prayer for kindness.

"Spread Your protection over them," he prays (v. 11, NIV). But take note. This isn't just any kind of protection. The Passion translation describes this particular protection as a "canopy of kindness" (v. 12).

Oh, sweet Jesus. Can you feel the shade? The breeze? The hush of anything harsh? David is crying for coverage. And the coverage is a canopy. And the canopy is kindness.

What a necessary provision when life feels raw and we are too much pelted by grief, anger, and fear. Too susceptible to that which falls down, bears down, and beats down all harsh and hard.

God's coverage is a canopy, and the canopy is kindness. Yes. Amen.

David not only prayed for a canopy of kindness; he created one too. Long after his friend Jonathan's death, David inquired, "Is there anyone still left of the house of Saul [Jonathan's father, who sought to kill David] to whom I can show kindness for Jonathan's sake?" (2 Sam. 9:1, NIV).

And it turned out there was. A son of Jonathan's by the name of Mephibosheth, a man who was lame in both of his feet.

King David had him brought to his residence, where he would eat at the king's table each day. Not only that, but David restored to Mephibosheth all of the land that had belonged to his grandfather, Saul. A canopy of kindness to protect and provide.

The truth is, we can spread hate, spread fear, and spread rumors, living under them and growing darker each day. Or we can spread kindness. Stretch it straight out, as a safe shelter in so many storms.

God's coverage is a canopy, and the canopy is kindness.

In all that's bearing down and beating down upon our hearts and heads, cover us, O God. Be our shelter, our safety, our shade. Show us no little kindness. Instead, spread it wide so we can hide. We rest ourselves in you.

PONDER

Recall a time someone extended kindness to you in even the smallest of ways. Write or tell someone about it in detail, including its impact on you.

PRACTICE

Ask the question King David posed: "To whom can I show the kindness of God?" Make it a practice to ask this question at the start of each day this week. Act on what you hear.

PRAY

Cover and keep me under your canopy of kindness, O God.

44

HUSH NOW

PRAYER: *Calm the chaos in me.*

The disciples were in a boat on the lake when their "storm formed" (Mark 4:37, VOICE).

How about you? What little piece of life were you going about when your storm formed?

Maybe you saw it brewing, looming, gathering strength in the distance. Maybe you knew to expect it, heard its forecast. Maybe not. Maybe it descended with no time for screaming sirens, catching you completely unaware. It doesn't really matter. The point is, the wind whipped. The waves crashed. And that vessel that held you was suddenly swamped and sinking fast.

If our experience is anything akin to the disciples', we find that the storm without quickly becomes a storm within. Our emotions rise and fall in rhythm with the wind-whipped waves.

Meanwhile, back in the boat, Jesus is asleep in the stern.

They wake him, the disciples do, and he speaks to the storm. Says things like:

- Quiet! Be still!
- Hush! Be muzzled!
- That's enough!
- Settle down!

I'm wondering: Jesus, are you speaking to the wind and waves or to the disciples themselves? Because I need you to say those words to me. I need you to stand up and speak into the chaos in me; I can't think straight when all is noise and rage. I need Your command:

- Hush now.
- That's enough.
- Settle down.

I used to be a bit irritated and angry by Jesus's sleepiness at a time like that. I now see he was the only one unmoved by the storm, and that's not a bad thing. His anchor held. For everyone else, their inner life took on the same feel of all that raged around them (as too often does mine!). Because they were swept up in the storm, the disciples lost their power to speak to the storm. All they could do was feed its intensity.

Not so for Jesus. Unlike us (or at least me), his inner state of peace and trust held. And through that holding, he was able to affect the outer state of the storm. He brought calm, not chaos. Rooted in peace, he was able to bring peace and speak peace.

"And the wind died down [as if it had grown weary] and there was [at once] a great calm [a perfect peacefulness]" (Mark 4:39, AMP).

Oh Jesus, it's windy down here! Everything's whipped into overwhelm, and it feels like the lot of us are swamped and sinking fast. Do something! Say something! Stand and command something—the wind, the waves, my wearied soul. When you stand up, our fears sit down. May our winds become weary and our chaos grow calm.

PONDER

Name a recent storm that formed in your life. In what ways did you react or respond?

PRACTICE

Make a storm emergency kit, but in this case fill it with items that help to ground and settle you down. What might you put in it?

PRAY

Wind whisperer, calm the chaos in me.

45

REST WELL

PRAYER: I rest myself in you.

I have COVID-19—*again*—and it's kicking my sweet little hiney. I haven't showered in four, or possibly five, days. Due to the constant coughing spasms and sneezing fits, I haven't slept either.

But here I am in my morning prayer room. "What am I even doing here," I wonder. No long prayers. No Scripture studies. No ability to engage in deep listening.

It's barely light outside. Why am I not still in bed?

And then I realize. I just want to be in the place of God's presence. In the place of God's peace. In the place of God's protection and my own eventual prospering. And for me, that occurs in my prayer room more than any other place.

I think of the psalmist's longing for the same: To be in God's house. To sit down in the shadow of Shaddai. I resonate with his words when he says, "Whoever dwells in the shelter of the Most High will rest in the shadow of the

Almighty. I will say of the LORD, 'He is my refuge and my fortress, my God, in whom I trust'" (Ps. 91:1–2, NIV).

I long to take refuge in God until this storm passes.

And I'm struck by the beginning of the psalmist's words: "Whoever dwells in the shelter . . . rests." Rest is just what the doctor ordered for the healing of my body, but my tired soul aches for the same. Whoever dwells, rests.

When I can't find rest for my body, I know where to find rest for my soul.

I can't be productive right now, but I can be presenced, and perhaps that is the best gift of all. Perhaps that's all that is needed. I can keep company with him who keeps me.

So here I am. I want to put myself in the place of God's care. Where the God of all comfort keeps me still and carries me through. If I need to hide, I want to hide here, in the hollows of the God who holds me.

God, tell us once more that your love for us does not depend on our productivity. That when we have nothing to offer, you still offer yourself. Receive us just as we are, and presence us through.

PONDER

Do you have a physical location (like my prayer room or the temple of old) that represents God's presence to you?

How is it for you to approach God with nothing at all to offer?

What inhibits your ability to simply rest in God?

PRACTICE

Rest in God's presence. Period. Do nothing other than allowing yourself to be held and be loved.

PRAY

God of all comfort, I rest myself in you.

WELL AND WHOLE

PRAYER: Make me well and whole.

I was recovering from that second round of COVID and was scheduled to fly, within days, to another state for meetings and to help facilitate a retreat.

I was no longer contagious and probably, possibly, feasibly was well enough to go.

Well enough means reasonably acceptable, passable, fairly satisfactory.

Should I have left *well enough* alone and gone on the trip? Muddled through? In the past, I would have—but to the detriment of me. I have a pretty solid track record of leaving well enough alone. Of making do and getting by.

Jesus isn't interested in well enough, though. Take the story where he healed the blind man. Upon the first try, the blind man said, "I see people; they look like trees walking around" (Mark 8:24, NIV). At this point, Jesus could have left well enough alone. The man recovered some sight, so let's call it a win.

But he did no such thing. Instead, Jesus brought this man all the way through to completion, to wholeness, to health. Putting his hands on the man's eyes once again, Jesus prayed until "his sight was restored, and he saw everything clearly" (v. 25, NIV).

Completion, wholeness, and health. In the Scriptures, these are the words used to describe the concept of perfection.

When the apostle James wrote to the suffering saints of his day, he encouraged them to "let perseverance finish its work so that [they] may be mature and complete, not lacking anything" (Jas. 1:4, NIV). The Amplified Bible says, "So that you may be [people] perfectly and fully developed" (AMPC).

Perfectly and fully. That isn't well enough but well and whole. And according to James, it's worth waiting for, worth staying in process with, as Jesus works it out over time.

This perfectionism is not that of crossing your t's and dotting your i's. That's the easy variety, if you ask me. This, rather, is bringing something or someone to fullness. And it's often, as James described it, a work of waiting and of staying in the game. A perfection born of patient perseverance.

What if we asked for this? (Goodness, that would be brave!) What if we didn't leave well enough alone anymore but rather went all the way through to completion, to wholeness, to health? To the richest measure there may be? What if we submitted ourselves to the full work of God for the sake of ourselves, our neighbors, our world?

What if we waited on well and whole?

Help us, God, to stay in the process. To stay with you. To not give up halfway through. Finish what you started. Bring us all the way through.

PONDER

What does it feel like to let God "finish a work" in you, bringing it all the way through?

For what reasons and in what areas of your life do you settle for, or possibly prefer, leaving well enough alone?

How might God be inviting you to cooperate with him in bringing wellness and wholeness into your life, work, community, world?

PRACTICE

Bring something, anything, all the way through to completion.

PRAY

God, do your full work of grace in me. Make me well and whole.

47

FULL STOP

PRAYER: *Lead me to rest.*

My son is an athlete, and movement is his medicine. Movement is also his job. Whether he's training for his own races, helping to coach a cross country team, or serving as a wellness specialist at a local retirement community, movement marks his days from beginning to end.

So when the orthopedic doctor recommended he make a full stop, he felt the ground quake under his chronically injured foot.

Our son has been injured for well over a year and, for good reason, has spent an exorbitant amount of time, energy, and money looking for a fix. He longs for a green light and go-lane to get back on his feet.

It turns out, though, that sometimes instead of pressing on or pushing through, instead of finding fixes in order to move forward, a full stop is what we need.

No weight-bearing, the doctor said, not even in the boot

he'd be wearing for six weeks. No standing. No walking. No running back and forth in the boot to cheer on his team. Full stop. The pressure needs to be taken off in order to heal.

Allow me to repeat that: The pressure needs to be taken off in order to heal.

Like my son, I resist a full stop. It's inconvenient when all I want is to carry on. It's terrible for my ego and terrifying to my fears.

In the lexicon of punctuation, a full stop is a period—the dot at the end of a sentence. The spot we sit upon as we wait for the next words to appear. It is a holding place, a hard place, and, as it turns out, a healing place. A place that not only the orthopedist but God would recommend: sabbaths, sabbaticals, seven-year rests.

"In returning and rest, you will be saved," God's prophet told God's people. "In quietness and trust you will find strength. But you refused. You couldn't sit still" (Isa. 30:15–16, VOICE).

Stopping can be scary, but it's sacred. Taking the pressure off is a prescription for our healing. Full stops are how we roll.

Lead us, God, to periods of rest. Not as a rebuke but for restoration and repair. For the healing of all that's worn thin, worn down, worn away. For ourselves and those around us and the very soil on which we stand.

PONDER

When has rest been forced upon you, and how did you respond?

Do you refuse rest, and if so, why?

What, if anything, steals your rest or makes it difficult for you to enter into it?

PRACTICE

In working up to full stops, try mini ones by pausing for thirty seconds in between tasks throughout your day. Take a deep, intentional breath. Stretch. Do a little dance. Say a little prayer. Pause before pivoting to what is next.

Engage in a regular rhythm of rest. If you can't take twenty-four hours off each week, try for one very intentional hour and go from there. Turn off your devices, gaze on beauty, move your body, feast with friends. Take the pressure off.

PRAY

Good Shepherd, lead me to rest, and restore my soul.

48

SAY WHEN

PRAYER: *Teach me to say when.*

My husband tells a story of his first time in France. It was a Sunday, and his day began by attending a large church in Germany, where he was invited to a feast of a meal following the service.

Four hours later, he arrived in France, still quite full. Little did he know his host family had spent the day preparing a traditional seven-course meal to welcome him!

Unsuspecting of what lay ahead, he ate the two pieces of quiche he was served as the meal began. That was cleared away and he thought he was done, but the meal went an additional three and a half hours.

Out came the soup and bread. Then the homemade pasta and meat. After those were cleared away, salad was placed on his plate. Then cheeses, followed by fruit and nuts.

By the time this was all topped off with coffee and cookies, my dear husband was literally bursting at the seams. He said he was so uncomfortable he could not lie down to sleep.

All he could do was pace the hallways, back and forth and back once more.

It reminds me of when I was a child and my parents would pour my drink or put food on my plate, instructing me to "say when." *When* meaning stop, no more, that's enough. It was my responsibility, my choice as to how much I allowed to fill my plate or cup. I was in charge of portion control.

These words are coming back to me now as I have a lot of options, like my husband's seven-course meal, that could be put on my plate: speaking engagements, writing opportunities, more spiritual direction clients to see. And I realize I'm not so good at saying *when*. At setting boundaries. At saying I can't possibly handle anything more right now because I'm so very full and it's getting uncomfortable and impossible to rest.

Saying *when* is particularly hard when we, like my husband, are offered such appetizing foods! I desire and enjoy almost all of what is being put on my plate, but there is too much of it. And too much of a good thing is still too much.

I wonder how my eyes might better listen to and honor my stomach or spirit so I don't swell in such an uncomfortable way.

Jesus, how did you know when to say when? How did you know when to say twelve disciples were enough? To say it was time to leave a certain town? To say no to more healings because you needed to go and pray? How did you know when to say when, when so many people put so much on your plate? Teach us, we pray.

PONDER

Think of a time when your plate was too full. How did it get that way?

Think of a time you said *when*. How did it feel, and what was the fruit of it?

PRACTICE

Draw a large circle. This is now your plate. Write on it all of the things that are "on your plate" in life right now. Size the words in proportion to how much space each one takes up in your life. Looking at your full plate, does anything surprise you or stand out to you? Do you have room for more? Does anything need to be rightsized?

PRAY

When my eyes are bigger than my stomach, teach me to say *when*.

CROP ROTATION

PRAYER: Replenish my soul's soil.

Lancaster, Pennsylvania, the land I call home, is full of farmers, and I am not one. That said, I've learned a practice from living in proximity to them: the practice of crop rotation.

Crop rotation is exactly what it sounds like. It is when farmers, instead of planting the same thing over and over again, sow different crops on the very same soil. Rotating the crops prevents the same nutrients from being drawn out of the ground time and again. Mixing it up improves the health of the soil, optimizes its nutrients, and has the added benefit of combating weeds.

Life in the soil thrives on variety. When's the last time you mixed it up a bit?

I know from my athletic son that doing the same physical exercises over and over again is rather pointless. You need to mix it up to gain the full benefit. It makes me wonder what ruts I've gotten into and if any of my routines could use a little rotating. I'm thinking here of my diet, exercise, spiritual practices, daily schedule, work life, and relationships.

What new things might nourish?

It's not just crops that need rotating. Tires do too. I read that by doing so, it helps them wear evenly. It reduces drag, extends their life, and can even prevent blowouts. Hello!

In the spirit of all this, I rotate some work crops each year. I take two months off from my regular jobs to engage in larger creative projects. While I plan some vacation during this time, it's more about rotation than rest.

I'm feeling a tug to rotate other areas as well, especially in my spiritual practices. I typically relate to God through words (mine and his), so in order to rotate, I just ordered a resource to help me engage in art as well.

We can rotate in big or small ways. Think about how you spend your free time or what type of books you typically read. Consider trying new foods, an alternate route to work, or a different way of relating to a loved one.

God, when I'm stuck in a rut, prompt me to rotate. May my soul's soil be replenished and balanced, so as to sustain life with new vigor and vim!

PONDER

In which routines, rituals, or relationships do you feel stuck in a rut?

What might you rotate in order to replenish?

PRACTICE

Try doing one thing in a different way for a three-week
period of time.

PRAY

Creative God, replenish my soul's soil.

CULTIVATE OR CUT DOWN

PRAYER: *Show me what to cultivate and what to cut down.*

Long, long ago, in the land where I still live, we planted a tree in our front yard. A plum tree. It was pretty. It provided shade. And it fell over every single time a storm blew through. It didn't just bend; it literally fell over, trunk to the ground.

With neighborly help, we rescued our tree each time. We dug the hole deeper, staked it to the ground, trimmed off the top-heavy branches. And still it fell. How long would we have compassion on this tree?

This reminds me of the parable Jesus told in Luke 13. In this story we meet a tree, a gardener, and the owner of a vineyard. The tree, similar to ours, was experiencing some difficulty in its little life. For three years, the owner came looking for fruit on it, only to find none. "Cut it down!" he said. "Why should it use up the soil?"

The gardener, however, had a different idea. Instead of cutting it down, he suggested they cultivate it. "'Sir,' the man replied, 'leave it alone for one more year, and I'll dig around it and fertilize it'" (v. 8, NIV).

As you might have guessed, I'm a great fan of the gardener. I jump for joy with a shout of hallelujah over the mercy and kindness he shows to the tree.

But I completely (and conveniently?) ignore his final words: "If it bears fruit next year, fine! If not, then cut it down" (v. 9, NIV).

What? No! Permission to cut the tree down? Never!

In all fairness, the owner of the vineyard had a legitimate question when he asked, "Why waste good ground with it any longer?" (v. 7, MSG).

I notice there was no guarantee, even after a year of specialized care from the gardener, the tree would live up to its potential. There remained a possibility it would go on depleting the soil and blocking the sunlight, negatively impacting the other trees. A possibility it might have to be cut down after all.

I sense an invitation to view this whole scenario differently. Instead of seeing the owner as the bad guy who shows no mercy, might I view him as the one who has the fuller picture in mind? The longer view? The health of the whole as a priority?

Can I see the fruitless tree's removal as a gift and a grace that provides space for what is living or what wants to come forth? Is what feels so hostile to me actually an act of hospitality?

God, I welcome you not only as the gardener who cultivates, cares for, nourishes, and nurtures, but also as the owner, who, for the sake of the whole, knows when to cut out, cut down, or carry away. God, have mercy on the tree of me.

PONDER

What is taking up too much space in the vineyard of you or
your work?

Is there a tree to which you're giving undue attention, trying
to keep it alive when its time has passed or simply may never
come?

Is your attachment to that particular tree a hindrance to the
health of the vineyard as a whole?

PRACTICE

Survey the things to which you are giving your time and
effort. Write them down, pray about them, talk with a friend,
and consider: Is there anything whose time has come to go?

PRAY

God of the long view, show me what to cultivate and what to
cut down.

51

HEED. HEEL.

PRAYER: *Help me to heed. Help me to heel.*

E very now and then, my spirit prays something my mind hasn't yet considered. When it happens, I know to pay attention, and it happened last week. I was praying in the early morning hours when I heard myself say, "Help me to heed," followed closely by "Help me to heel."

The image that accompanied this prayer was that of dog training. Lacking any experience in this, because we only had a pet dog for a matter of months when I was a child, I did a deeper dive into the meaning of these words.

To *heed* means to pay attention, take notice of, and give careful consideration to. No surprise there.

However, I was all wrong about the meaning of *heel*. (Do not let me train your dogs!) I thought it meant "Sit! Stay!" But I came to find out it means to follow closely behind someone —to stay at their heels. Not being a fan of either sitting or staying, I warmed well to this new insight.

The words *heed* and *heel* have become my invitation and

reminder to listen to God's voice and stay by God's side. To not run ahead, but rather to move when God moves, go where God goes, stay where God stays. Heed. Heel. Here. Now.

There is a great deal of freedom in this, in trusting that all will be provided and I need not chase after anything. It's where I want to be, especially when I don't know where to go, what to do, or what to say.

I believe this is similar to Jesus's relationship with the Father. Jesus, who said he only did what he saw the Father doing and only spoke what he heard the Father saying (John 5:19; 12:49). He heeded. He heeled. Jesus stayed close to the Father's side.

Heed. Heel.
Stay close by my side,
your foot to my step,
your eyes to my hand,
your ear to my voice,
your head to my heart.
Heed. Heel.
Stay close by my side.

God, we chase after so many squirrels! We can be such a distracted lot, running ahead, lagging behind, and wasting all kinds of energy while doing so. All we need is found in you. You are our companion and guide. Help us to follow your lead.

PONDER

How might the invitation to heed and heel be for your protection and peace?

What squirrels do you chase, and why?

PRACTICE

Watch a video on training a dog to heel. What do you notice? Journal about it or discuss it with friends or family.

PRAY

Guiding God, help me to heed; help me to heel.

52

(K)NOT THIS DAY!

PRAYER: Untie me.

I can get myself tied in knots. Or more accurately, *nots*.
Not enough.
Not able.
Not equipped.
Not wanted.
(K)nots.

I become twisted, tangled, and tightened to that which restricts my reach.

I once read that knots weaken the rope in which they're made. That the bending and crushing that holds a knot in place causes stress and leads to a reduction in the strength of the rope. I'd venture to say my "nots" do the very same thing: create stress and reduce strength.

Once, when Jesus was in a synagogue on the Sabbath, he saw a woman who was knotted in pain, bent double for eighteen years. After calling her forward, Jesus posed a question to a group of religious leaders. "Can't we untie her?" he wanted to know. "Can't we loosen this knot and let her go? Can't we free her from that which inhibits her life?" (See Luke 13:10–16.)

Good question, Jesus.

There are all kinds of (k)nots untied in the Scriptures:

- Children, *not* significant enough to be included (Mark 10:13–16).
- Lepers, *not* clean enough to be touched (Luke 5:12–13).
- Widows, *not* rich enough to contribute (Mark 12:41–44).
- Tax collectors, *not* holy enough to be heard (Luke 18:9–14).
- Sinners, *not* worthy enough to be spared (John 8:1–11).
- Elizabeth, *not* young enough to bear children (Luke 1:5–25).
- David, *not* equipped enough to do battle (1 Sam. 17).
- Moses, *not* skilled enough to lead (Ex. 4:10–12).

(K)nots loosened and people let go.

We're told that when Jesus saw the woman doubled over in the synagogue, he called her over and gently laid his hands on her. "Dear woman," he said, "you are free. I release you forever from this crippling spirit" (Luke 13:13, TPT).

Released forever from the blasted (k)nots. Ties that bind in all the wrong ways.

Jesus, we're so (k)notted up. Tangled, tied, and tired. Untie us and let us go.

PONDER

What gets you all (k)notted up?

PRACTICE

Learn to tie a new knot (and to untie it too!).

Treat yourself to a massage to work out the knots you feel in your body. Allow the ones in your spirit to dissipate under the healing touch too.

Take your (k)notted-up self into the presence of Jesus. Feel the warmth of his gentle touch right on that (k)not. Feel it begin to loosen in his presence as he tells you, "You are free."

PRAY

Christ who came to set us free, please, oh please, untie me.

53

PATHS OF PAIN

PRAYER: *Come find me.*

I have a very challenged sense of direction. Unlike my husband, for whom it is nearly impossible to get lost, I know what it is to end up on roads I never intended to take. Roads that carry me far from where I want to be.

I was thinking about that this morning when I read the following prayer out of Psalm 139: "See if there is any path of pain I'm walking on," the psalmist asked of God, "and lead me . . . back to you" (v. 24, TPT).

Paths of pain. We end up on those sometimes, don't we? And most times, unintentionally so. Just as I don't purposely set out to get lost or stuck directionally, neither do I plan to travel a path of pain relationally. But both happen. And I often need help, like the psalmist, to find my way back home.

For me, the path of pain is often a false narrative I've wandered down. An untrue or only partially true story I spin about myself or others, about my situations or circumstances —and sometimes even about God.

They are like side trails on which we become disoriented and lost, bogged down by brambles and brush. But then again, I've been on some of those paths with such regularity, they've become well-worn, and I can confuse them entirely for the right road.

Regardless of what they look like, these paths of pain never take me where I want to go. Ever. They are consistent that way. They lead me to places like shame, isolation, and paralysis. They are, after all, paths of pain.

When I find myself on one of these, I, like the psalmist, need God to reroute me safely to the right road. But sadly, I don't always heed the directions or corrections that are given.

The prophet Jeremiah lets me know I'm not alone in this: "Go stand at the crossroads and look around. Ask for directions to the old road, the tried-and-true road. Then take it. Discover the right route for your souls" (Jer. 6:16, MSG).

If we stop reading there, Jeremiah's words sound lovely. Hopeful and reassuring. But that's not the end of the verse. It continues, revealing the people's defiant response: "But they said, 'Nothing doing. We aren't going that way.'"

Instead of heeding, they went headlong into harm.

I believe there is an intersection where the path of pain and the path of peace cross one another, and it is there we get to decide which road to take. A pause to position correctly, to choose our course, before continuing on.

Grant us, God, discernment to know where the road we are traveling on will lead us. Direct our steps into the paths of peace.

PONDER

What false narratives are paths of pain for you? Where do they lead you?

PRACTICE

Circle any of the following paths of pain you find yourself on: perfectionism, performance, people-pleasing, pride, pretension, panic, prejudice, possessiveness, presumption, predicting, proving, protecting, pushiness, pettiness, project-ing. What else might you add? Who is it hurting, and in what ways?

Purposefully get lost, then ask your GPS to get you home.

PRAY

Great Shepherd of the sheep, come find me.

54

TURNING POINTS

Prayer: Help me to follow you.

I was on a retreat when our facilitator led a group of us to a labyrinth and invited us to consider where, in these meandering paths, we found ourselves to be. Were we entering or exiting? Were we far-flung off to one side or nearing the center?

I didn't know.

All I knew was that I was at a place where the path turns. I was at a turning point.

To turn is to move something so it's in a different position, facing a different direction. And to turn toward one thing is to turn away from another. Herein lay my struggle. Yours too, maybe? I am too often attached to where I am.

Turning points are invitations to see and walk into something previously hidden from our sight. By their very nature, they are invitations to leave something behind: ways of seeing, ways of being, some beliefs, and even some griefs.

It's what happened when Jesus invited the fishermen to

follow him. "Come, follow Me," he told them, "and I will make you fishers of men" (Matt. 4:19, VOICE). It happened to Saul on the road to Damascus, when he went from persecuting the church to leading it (Acts 9). And it happened to the disciple Peter, when his beliefs about who and what were unclean were challenged and changed (Acts 10).

And it's happening now to me. An invitation to turn from my weeping years toward hope once more. To walk from all that has died, back into life.

One might think it would be easy to turn from mourning into dancing, but not so much. Not always.

Turning points reveal my attachments and my fears. I can get stuck in my old stories, in my former ways of being, seeing, behaving, or believing. Attached to who I was and apprehensive of what's to come.

But I'm at a turning point. And to turn is to change. And to change is to let something go. Like Peter, like Paul, like those early disciples of Jesus. Will we take our turn?

God, I know what was, and I know what is, and it feels safer to camp right here. I don't know what's around this bend. But here we are, and you beckon me on. Help me to take my turn.

PONDER

Where are you currently being invited to change? What resistances do you notice rising up within you? What fears?

Where are you stuck? What do you fear? And what do you need in order to "take your turn"?

Choose one of the stories of Peter, Paul, or the disciples, and notice what it must have cost them to "take their turn." Note also the fruit of their decision. What would the cost have been if they had chosen to stay where and how they were?

PRACTICE

Move a chair in your home or office to face a different way, see a different view.

Walk a labyrinth. Locate where you are on your journey right now.

Name one to three turning points you've experienced in your life. Pick one to journal about or to share with a friend.

PRAY

Help me to follow you, Jesus, through all the twists and turns in life.

55

EAR TO THE GROUND

PRAYER: Help me listen.

So very much happens below the surface of our individual, communal, and cultural lives. There are the seismic shifts that sometimes threaten to tear us asunder. But there are also the almost imperceptible sounds of hope, subtle stirrings harder to hear, of seeds sinking down, bulbs breaking open, roots reaching for one another in deep darkness.

I regret to say I don't always listen intently enough to hear any of this. I too often respond merely to what I see— which, of course, is never the whole story.

I once had a picture in my mind of Jesus on his hands and knees in the dirt. Bottom high and head low, ear to the ground of my life. In this image, he was not only listening to what was below the surface of me, but he was speaking to it as well. And in that gentle, quiet, tender way of his, he was coaxing it forth, inviting it to come to full light and life.

Oh, that we could do the same! That we, like Jesus, could

be present to the unseen, unsaid, unsurfaced questions or needs in our lives, the lives of others, and our very world.

What if, by bending low to listen—to ourselves, our sisters and brothers, or the Spirit of God—we could perceive what is happening below the surface? Perhaps then we could prevent, prepare for, partner with, or provide for what is truly needed.

Isn't that what the prophets of old did, time and again? Ears to the ground, listening to that which they could not see.

"Listen carefully," God says, "I am about to do a new thing. . . . Will you not be aware of it?" (Isa. 43:19, AMP).

God, with your ear to the ground of our lives, listen to the rumblings, the worries, and the concerns. Listen to our shame that we're too afraid to name. Listen us to freedom and out of all this fear. Listen us to hope and out of this despair. Listen to our longings; listen to our dreams; listen to all within us that is yet unnamed, unseen.

PONDER

What is happening below the surface of your life? What seismic shifts or subtle stirrings do you sense?

In what arena of your life are you being invited to listen more deeply?

PRACTICE

Go outside. Get down on all fours, bend down low, put your

ear to the ground, and listen. How can you bring that posture with you into your noisy days?

Sit in quiet for five minutes. Begin by praying the words Eli gave to Samuel: "Speak, LORD, for your servant is listening" (1 Sam. 3:9, NIV).

Take the above prayer and practice with you into conversations with others, starting with a posture of "Speak, [name], for I am listening."

PRAY

Attentive God, help me listen for that which I cannot see.

FEED YOUR FEARS

I t was crowded. It had probably been so for days on end, possibly weeks and months. So many people. So many needs. So little time. So much noise.

Enough is enough sometimes, or so Jesus seemed to say in this situation, as he invited his disciples to leave it all for a little alone time.

"Let's take a break and find a secluded place where you can rest a while," he said (Mark 6:31, TPT). I'm pretty sure his friends sighed as they slipped into their sailboat to reach that silent shore.

And then it happened, as it often did. The crowds caught on and began the chase on foot. And wouldn't you know it? "By the time Jesus came ashore, a massive crowd was waiting" (v. 34, TPT).

Are you feeling it? I am. But it's the internal crowds I'm referencing now. Mine are a motley mob made up of questions and concerns, of what-ifs and worries. Maybe your crowd contains grief or anger, regrets or failures, critical voices that follow you wherever you roam.

As I listen to mine, it's fear I hear. They're a noisy lot, this bunch, as they jostle for position, call for attention, push and press to get their needs met.

"You should send the crowds away," the disciples said to Jesus (v. 36, TPT), and I echo their sentiments 100 percent. We came here for quiet, not more chaos.

But Jesus called them to compassion. To have compassion on that which crowded them. *Oof*, Jesus!

He sat them down, these multitudes, in orderly fashion on patches of green. And he fed them full. Every last one.

I want Jesus to dismiss my fears and disperse them, but he dines with them instead. Jesus literally feeds my fears.

And I wonder if he's on to something, because he usually is. Might I have compassion on that which crowds me—the what-ifs and worries, the questions and concerns? Instead of trying to shoo them away or shut them out (which honestly makes them shout all the more), might I invite them to sit a spell instead? To settle down on a green patch of grass and be fed the faithfulness of God?

May we feed our fears, not so they will grow larger, but rather become satiated and settled, ready to be dismissed in peace.

Feed your fears, friend. Set a table for that which you can't outrun.

Jesus, there's so much we'd rather outrun. Give us the courage to have compassion on the crowds that keep coming so close.

PONDER

What crowds do you struggle to outrun, and how do you feel toward them?

What do you think they need to be fed in order to be dismissed in peace?

PRACTICE

On individual note cards or pieces of scrap paper, write down the things crowding you. Then lay out a picnic blanket and spread those papers out on it. Pick up one at a time and address it. Listen to what it has to say. Offer it care in any way you can.

PRAY

Feed my fears, God, with your great faithfulness.

57

PARTY CRASHERS

PRAYER: Crash my party!

I want a God who will wipe out the enemies that keep crashing my party. A God who will conquer them, please. No more sorrow or suffering. No more anxiety or fear. Hosanna to the God who will clear them away or act as a bouncer and keep them at bay.

But, alas, I get a God who not only lets them in but sets a table in their very presence (Ps. 23:5). I'm not entirely on board with this. I question the wisdom of this. This God exasperates me sometimes.

Enemies can be defined as those things which cause restriction, that put us into a tight place. Suffering, distress, oppression. I don't enjoy their company. Don't want to do life with them. They are not my invited guests. Someone should keep them out, don't you think?

One day the sorrow and sighing will be no more. I know this. One day joy will overtake them. One day they will flee away. But that day is not yet here—that much is clear. This day, if we are to feast, a table must be spread in the midst of them.

I want the absence of the hard. God gives me the presence of himself. He is a God who is in the midst. A God who doesn't wait to feast until all the beasts are gone. An audacious God who sets a table right there.

I wonder what might happen if I didn't bar them either. The enemies, that is. If, instead of expending all my energy trying to swat them out like so many dratted flies, I gave up on making things perfect before the party could commence. What might happen if I, like God, allowed them to come to the table as well? To share in the feast? Might they be comforted or calmed by what happens there?

Or here's a radical thought: What if it's not the enemies crashing our party but God crashing theirs? Yes! Setting a table right there in the shadows and sorrows. Laying out his feast in the middle of those fearsome foes!

God, we prefer doing life in the absence of our enemies, but you set a table in the presence of them. Maybe you're the wise one after all. Help us come to the table and feast, even here, even now, even with the company we'd rather not keep.

PONDER

Who or what keeps crashing your party?

What might it be like to sit down at the table, in God's presence, with the sorrow and suffering, anxieties or fears you would rather banish?

PRACTICE

Find one way to celebrate this week, even in a small way, even in the midst of all that is.

Plan an imaginary party. Draw up a guest list, and include at least some of your enemies—those things or people that put you in a tight place. What would your seating chart look like? Where would it take place—a hospital room, deathbed, unemployment office, a child's messy room? What would be on the menu? Imagine greeting each guest as they come, giving them a seat at the table, and sitting down with them. Imagine the interaction that unfolds.

PRAY

Crash my party, God!

58

BOUNCERS AND BLESSERS

Prayer: Bless me.

At the end of Jesus's time on Earth, we're told he led his disciples out as far as the town of Bethany, and "lifting up his hands, he blessed them" (Luke 24:50, NRSV).

Take a moment right now to open to what that may have felt like. The warmth of it. The healing. Especially considering this group of friends had just failed him, fled from him, and acted out of fear.

Most of Jesus's blessings involved his hands, which I picture as the large, strong hands of a carpenter but with a tender touch. I see his hands placed over the eyes of the blind, on the sweet heads of children, or pressed against the exposed skin of the leprous ones. I see them reaching down to raise and release an adulterous woman, stretched out to receive a drink from a Samaritan outcast, or used to restore the ear of the (perceived) enemy's servant.

And I see Jesus's hands holding Judas's feet—oh, reader—

washing and wiping them mere moments before his betrayal. I see his hands breaking bread and passing the cup, all for the life of others and us.

While Jesus sought to bless, there was often counter-movement from others, some in his own tight-knit Twelve, who sometimes served more as bodyguards and bouncers than blessers.

How often we do the same. We position ourselves as patrollers, seeking to protect. But who and what are we protecting? Surely not Jesus. More likely than not, it's our own agenda or theology, our ways, wants, or wishes.

We don't always get this right.

Once upon a time, the disciples sought to prevent children from coming to Jesus to receive his blessing. Can you imagine? They physically stood between him and the children. What a terrifying visual!

Eugene Peterson put Jesus's response to this occurrence in no uncertain terms: "The disciples shooed [the children] off. But Jesus was irate and let them know it: 'Don't push these children away. Don't ever get between them and me'" (Mark 10:13–14, MSG).

Let us be careful, friend, where we position ourselves. Jesus doesn't need bodyguards or bouncers who keep people out. He needs openers and ushers who bring them in. If we're going to position ourselves between others and Jesus, we ought to be opening the door, not closing it.

May nothing get between us and your blessing, Jesus. May nothing separate us from your love. May we come to you and not be turned away.

PONDER

What prevents you from coming to God? Is it a person, place, or thing? Ideology or theology? Rules or regulations? Policies or protocols? Shame, fear, pride, or pretense? Can you hear Jesus's voice inviting you, still?

Do you see yourself as a bouncer or blesser?

PRACTICE

Engage in some imaginative prayer. Put yourself into one of the stories above (Jesus blessing as he withdrew to heaven, Jesus washing Judas's feet, Jesus blessing the children). What character are you? Where do you find yourself in the story? How does it unfold? Linger there; don't rush. What do you notice? What do you feel?

As you leave interactions with others this week, quietly or silently whisper, "The Lord bless you."

PRAY

Bless me and keep me, dear God.

59

EACH DAY, ENOUGH

PRAYER: *Give me enough.*

How do you live with something? I'm talking about a debilitation, a diagnosis, a disease—a situation or circumstance that's difficult, day in and day out. How do you live with it, in it, through it?

A new friend of mine wanted to know just that. "How do you do it?" she asked.

How, indeed?

I pondered. I prayed. I wondered if I had anything of value to tell her. And then I remembered: *Each day, enough.*

I first encountered these words in the middle of Jesus's longest recorded public talk, when he began to address the theme of worry. After acknowledging the basic daily needs of his listeners, he moved from discussing their todays into their tomorrows. "Do not worry about tomorrow," Jesus told them, "for tomorrow will worry about itself. *Each day has enough* trouble of its own" (Matt. 6:34, emphasis added, NIV).

Jesus, ever the realist. *Each day, enough*, he said. Can I get an amen?

However, as if today isn't trouble enough, I have a tendency to make the hard even harder by dragging my yesterdays in. Piling them on, I'm pressed down by the accumulated weight of their griefs and grievances, troubles and trials, faults and failures.

Then, just for good measure (because why not?), I add my tomorrows to the mix. I borrow the burdens of the future through practices of what-ifs and worries.

None of this is recommended. I eventually made up a mantra to help myself stop the madness: "Don't borrow from tomorrow. Don't stay in yesterday. Each day, enough."

Then I realized a beautiful thing: It's not just the problems that are each day, enough. (Praise be!) The provisions are as well, and their names are *mercy* and *manna*.

Scripture tells us God's mercies, tender-kindness, love, and compassion are new every morning, and each day, enough (Lam. 3:22–23). God's manna, our daily bread, is as well. That which sustains us through the demands of our days is new every morning, and each day, enough.

How do you live with, live in, live through all the things? By returning time and again to each day, enough.

Release us, God, from our fear of the future and our focus on the past. Give us this day our daily bread, mercy and manna, both. Sustain our souls, we pray.

PONDER

In what ways do you borrow from tomorrow or stay in yesterday?

How do you live with, live in, or live through all that life brings?

PRACTICE

When you go to prayer, turn your hands down (maybe even shake them loose a bit) and release your fear of the future or your focus on the past. Then turn your palms face up, extending your hands to God, as you ask for today's portion of mercy and manna. Throughout the day, use the hand motions as a simple, wordless body prayer that returns you to the present provisions.

Join me in using my mantra as a way of returning your soul to a centered place: "Don't borrow from tomorrow. Don't stay in yesterday. Each day, enough."

PRAY

Gracious provider, give me enough.

60

RENEWABLE RESOURCES

PRAYER: Renew me.

While communing with God this morning, I caught myself anxiously praying about all that lay ahead for me, some of which has been staring me down and spinning me silly. That's when I sensed the Holy Spirit, like an anchor to my soul, drawing me back down into this day, this hour, this precious moment in time and God's great faithfulness to meet the needs.

All will be given.

Those were the words sent to settle my stirred-up soul. In fact, those are the words the Spirit has been whispering to me for several weeks now, most likely in the hope that one day soon they'll finally reach the roots of me. *All will be given. Open, dear daughter. Do not fear. Trust in the care of God.*

It's been a lot over here lately. Like an anxious chipmunk, I've found myself scurrying about, trying to stuff my cheeks full, stashing supplies for the season to come. I've been asking the God of daily bread for graces I don't yet need.

Trying to hoard all the help I can find out of fear it'll run plumb dry. As if God's mercies could ever end.

They cannot. We know this, right?

"Certainly the faithful love of the LORD hasn't ended; certainly God's compassion isn't through! They are *renewed every morning*" (Lam. 3:22–23, emphasis added, CEB).

They are renewed every morning, the writer said. They'll never run out. Can you imagine? A renewable resource is that which is not depleted when used. That which is naturally replenished at a rate that matches or exceeds its use.

We do not find the writer of Lamentations scrambling about and storing up scraps when faced with unimaginable need. Rather, we find him relying on the renewable resources of God's faithful love, compassion, and care.

Jesus taught about this too. When a group that gathered on a hillside was worked up and worried about their daily needs, he directed their thoughts to the birds, to the flowers, and then to their heavenly Father, who tends them both.

"Look at the birds in the sky," he said. "They do not store food for winter. . . . And yet, they are always fed because your heavenly Father feeds them. . . . If He looks after them, of course He will look after you" (Matt. 6:26, VOICE).

Of course he will. Be still, my sweet, scampering soul.

God, our resources are not always renewable, our reserves not always full. Out of your graces, grant us fresh supply.

PONDER

Which of your resources currently feel depleted?

What fears send you scurrying about in an effort to store up for what is to come?

What, if anything, makes it difficult for you to trust in the care of God?

PRACTICE

Sunlight is one source of renewable energy. This week, find ten minutes to sit in sunshine as you ask God to renew those places in you that feel depleted.

PRAY

God of endless supply, renew me.

ACKNOWLEDGMENTS

This book began with a deep bow, and I'd like to end it with one as well—a deep bow of thanks.

Christianne Squires, dear editor and friend, I loved you the moment I met you. I'm so grateful for the ways you see me and draw both me and my words out. You are pure gift!

This book would not exist apart from our Little Life Words community of readers on Substack. Thank you for receiving my words over these past five years and the encouragement you've offered. We did this together.

The very first seeds of this book were planted during the days of LiveWell!Ministries and our R&R Retreats. To those of you in this come-unity, know that your lives shaped mine in the most beautiful of ways. I love you forever and always.

Bookwifery friends (Becky, Anne, Kathy, Kathryn, Jen, Cindy, Melynne, Janice, Elisabeth, and Lisa), thank you for walking me through years of iterations and ideas. What compassionate, creative comrades you have been!

Heartfelt thanks to Nooks Bookstore in Lancaster, PA, for nurturing the kind of community that fosters creativity, and to our Artist's Way book club that increased my courage for all kinds of pursuits.

I want to express my gratitude to Jonathan and Jennie Groff for opening your AirBnB to me for a writing retreat. Those days away (and that deep-soak bathtub!) nourished me to reach the finish line.

Tracey Knauss, Cheryl Hollinger, and Kristen Esch, thank you, friends, for loving me well, praying me through, and sending me memes when I needed them most! What would I do without you?

Deep bow to my family. To Mom, for telling me your stories and believing in mine. To Ryan, for listening to way more mini sermons than a son should have to bear and for lending me your courage when I couldn't find my own. And to my dear husband, Dan, for reading, rereading, and reading some more. Your belief in and tireless support of me are bar none. I know how fortunate I am!

I could not close this book without honoring my tenth great-grandfather, Paul Gerhardt, a people's pastor and prolific poet from 1600s Germany, who I believe prayed for his descendants like me. I'm grateful to have gleaned so much goodness and grace from his life.

And finally, dear, sweet God, giver of every good gift and faithful through and through, I bow to you.

ABOUT THE AUTHOR

Jenny Gehman is a spiritual director, retreat facilitator, and freelance writer. Having spent more than two decades in a ministry of hospitality to international college students, Jenny is passionate about the wild, wide-open, warmhearted welcome of God, whom she names as our "Holy Host."

As the former founder and director of LiveWell!Ministries and R&R Retreats, Jenny is a seasoned speaker with experience in leadership development, retreat planning, and community cultivation. This experience serves her well in her current role as the East Coast representative for Mennonite Women USA, a role that affords her the opportunity to lift up the voices and uphold the value of women in their various roles.

Jenny served as a columnist for *Anabaptist World* magazine for five years and is a regular contributor to *Rejoice!* magazine. Her words can be found in a variety of books and blogs, as well as in her Little Life Words, which she publishes on a biweekly basis on Substack.

Jenny resides in the Amish country of Pennsylvania with her husband and a gaggle of guests. She enjoys crackling fires, classical music, and chocolate of the darkest variety.

Learn more or contact Jenny at www.jennygehman.com.

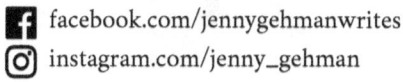

facebook.com/jennygehmanwrites
instagram.com/jenny_gehman

www.ingramcontent.com/pod-product-compliance
Lightning Source LLC
Chambersburg PA
CBHW021627120626
46545CB00002B/433